THE

APOSTOLIC FATHERS

A New Translation and Commentary

THE APOSTOLIC FATHERS

A New Translation and Commentary

edited by Robert M. Grant

University of Chicago

Volume 1   An Introduction
by Robert M. Grant, University of Chicago

Volume 2   First and Second Clement
by Robert M. Grant, University of Chicago
and Holt H. Graham, Virginia Theological Seminary

Volume 3   Barnabas and The Didache
by Robert A. Kraft, University of Pennsylvania

Volume 4   Ignatius of Antioch
by Robert M. Grant, University of Chicago

Volume 5   Polycarp, Martyrdom of Polycarp, Fragments of Papias
by William R. Schoedel, Brown University

Volume 6   Hermas
by Graydon F. Snyder, Bethany Theological Seminary

THE
APOSTOLIC FATHERS

A New Translation and Commentary

Volume 4

Ignatius of Antioch

by

Robert M. Grant

THOMAS NELSON & SONS

London   CAMDEN, N.J.   *Toronto*

PREFACE

Since the seventeenth century, when the authentic letters of
Ignatius were recovered (on the early transmission of the letters,
see my article, "The Apostolic Fathers' First Thousand Years,"
in *Church History* 31 [1962], 421-429)—thanks to the efforts of
the Reformed pastor Vedelius, the Anglican archbishop Ussher,
and the Dutch philologist Voss—they have provided materials for
two kinds of approaches. On the one hand, students have used
them to support theories of decline and fall in post-exilic Christianity; on the other, they have used them to illustrate continuity
in spite of modifications. The latter approach is generally followed in this translation and commentary, and it seems to be
justified by the primary method employed, that of interpreting
Ignatian passages in the context of (1) his own letters, (2) the
Pauline epistles, some of which he knew exceedingly well, and
(3) the kind of thought reflected above all in the Gospel of John.
Though other influences are certainly present (Gnostic or proto-
Gnostic, Hellenistic rhetorical, and, at second remove, Jewish)
these are not as important as the basic contexts we have
mentioned.

We hope that the commentary indicates both what Ignatius
said and what he meant, and that readers will share some of our
enthusiasm for an early Christian writer who has been admired
by both Nygren and Bultmann.

Robert M. Grant

CONTENTS

PREFACE v

CITATIONS AND ABBREVIATIONS ix

Introduction 1

Doctrine of God 5

Christology 7

Martyrdom 13

Faith and Eschatology 16

Spirit and Flesh 19

Church and Ministry 20

The Heresies and the Sources of Ignatius' Ideas 22

Criticism of Ignatius 25

EPHESIANS 27

Outline 28

Translation and Commentary 29

MAGNESIANS 55

Outline 56

Translation and Commentary 57

TRALLIANS 69

Outline 70

Translation and Commentary 71

ROMANS 83

Outline 84

Translation and Commentary 85

PHILADELPHIANS 97

Outline 98

Translation and Commentary   99

                          SMYRNAEANS   111
Outline   112
Translation and Commentary   113

                          POLYCARP   127
Outline   128
Translation and Commentary   129

Selected List of Editions   139
Selected Bibliography   141

CITATIONS AND ABBREVIATIONS

References to and citations from the Old Testament are usually made on the basis of the Greek version called the Septuagint (abbreviated LXX), and for this reason the meaning as well as the chapter and verse division will often differ from the Hebrew or the English translations.

The writings of the Apostolic Fathers are given the following abbreviations:

Barn.	Epistle of Barnabas
1 Clem.	Clement of Rome to the Corinthians
2 Clem.	2 Clement (sermon)
Did.	The Didache
Eph.	Ignatius to the Ephesians
Magn.	Ignatius to the Magnesians
Mand.	Hermas, Mandates
Mart. Polyc.	Martyrdom of Polycarp
Phil.	Polycarp to the Philippians
Philad.	Ignatius to the Philadelphians
Polyc.	Ignatius to Polycarp
Rom.	Ignatius to the Romans
Sim.	Hermas, Similitudes
Smyrn.	Ignatius to the Smyrnaeans
Trall.	Ignatius to the Trallians
Vis.	Hermas, Visions

In addition, the following abbreviations occur:

A.-G.	*A Greek-English Lexicon of the New Testament and Other Early Christian Literature. A translation and adaptation of Walter Bauer's Griechisch-Deutsches Wörterbuch zu den Schriften des Neuen Testaments und der*

übrigen urchristlichen Literatur (4th revised and augmented edition, 1952). By William F. Arndt and F. Wilbur Gingrich. Chicago, 1957.

Ad Autol.	Theophilus, *Ad Autolycum*
Adv. haer.	Irenaeus, *Adversus haereses*
Ancor.	Epiphanius, *Ancoratus*
Bell.	Josephus, *Bellum Iudaicum*
Ep.	*Epistles* (by various authors)
Exc. ex Theod.	Clement, *Excerpta ex Theodoto*
H.E.	Eusebius, *Historia Ecclesiastica*
Ioh. comm.	Origen, *In Iohannem commentarius*
Opif.	Philo, *De Opificio mundi*
PG	J. P. Migne, *Patrologia Graeca*
Princ.	Origen, *De Principiis*
Str.	Clement, *Stromata*

THE

APOSTOLIC FATHERS

A New Translation and Commentary

INTRODUCTION

The letters of Ignatius, Christian bishop of Antioch and martyr early in the second century, possess perennial importance because of (1) his vivid and ardent personality, more clearly delineated than that of any other early Christian but the apostle Paul, (2) his intense devotion to the unity of the Christian Church and his insistence upon the office of the bishop as the center of this unity, (3) his emphasis on the sacraments, especially the Eucharist, as mediating the life of the risen Lord to the community, and (4) his deep concern for the appropriation of the Lord's sacrificial death by means of the Christian's own martyrdom.

Ignatius' personality is reflected in his style. Though he was evidently trained in the dramatic Asianic rhetoric of his time, he was not concerned with rhetoric for its own sake but as a means for laying emphasis on the various aspects, especially the more paradoxical aspects, of the gospel which he had found most adequately expressed in the letters of Paul and in the teaching ascribed to John. His own letters are crowded with allusions to those of Paul, and he takes these letters to be addressed to himself. He relives Paul's life and identifies himself with the lives and deaths of both Paul and Jesus. By so doing he hopes that he himself, like Paul, will become a sacrificial offering on behalf of the Church.

In ancient times his letters were frequently regarded as inadequately orthodox, and in the fourth century they were drastically revised so that they would be more like the Pastoral Epistles and the writings of the other Apostolic Fathers. His devotion to Jesus Christ as his God seemed excessive; his neglect of the New Testament Gospels seemed strange. In times more modern he has often been criticized for (1) his exaltation of the episcopal office, (2) his concern with the Eucharist, (3) his determination to become a martyr and thus to "reach God," and (4) his comparative neglect of such matters as the doctrine of God as creator and governor of history and, consequently, the doctrine of Christ's imminent return. Critics have found a startling gap between

1

Ignatius and Paul and, indeed, between Ignatius and New Testament Christianity as a whole. They have regretted his lack of
apocalyptic eschatology, his insistence upon order at the expense
of freedom, his sacramental concerns, and his glorification of
martyrdom. They have often claimed that he does not understand
the Pauline views of either faith or grace.

/ In order to explain the differences between Ignatius' ideas and
those of Paul or John or Jesus, they have pointed either toward
his own psyche or toward the Hellenistic religious environment
in which, as a Christian at Antioch, he must have lived. The most
severe critic of Ignatius' psyche seems to have been B. H. Streeter,
partly because he was concerned with making contemporary
Christianity psychologically respectable.[1] In his view Ignatius
provided a classical case of the martyr complex, obsessed not by
God or by Christ but by a thoroughly neurotic death-wish. Evidence for this judgment was provided by Ignatius' letter to the
Romans, in which he explicitly says that he desires to die and
that he will entice the wild beasts to eat him but, on the other
hand, describes the torments that await him in language that
verges on the gruesome. Here a more impartial understanding of
Ignatius' situation may point toward a more favorable judgment.
He knows that he has been condemned to death and that for
Romans who were not citizens such deaths were indeed merciless.
Though the Roman Christians might somehow get him released,
his condemnation has provided him with the supreme opportunity to imitate the fidelity of Paul, the Paul who in turn (as
Ignatius knows) imitated Jesus. In Jesus, Ignatius will arise free,
not by virtue of what Roman Christians may do through political
influence of some sort. For him to escape death would be to betray not only those who preceded him from Syria to Rome for
God's glory but also the Christians from Antioch to Troas who
have "refreshed" him as a martyr-to-be; above all, it would be
to betray himself and his relationship to Christ. To say that
Ignatius is psychologically "normal" would be false. He lives in
a state of extreme tension between his fears of being untrue to
the work of God and his human anxiety about his fate. But to
criticize him as simply neurotic would be to reduce human existence to a level far below its potential heights. /

The second kind of explanation often provided for the differences between Ignatius and the New Testament is usually

[1] *The Primitive Church* (New York, 1929).

based upon (1) the selection of some of the more vividly imaginative passages in his letters and (2) the comparison of these
with other passages derived from or supposedly related to (a)
the Graeco-Oriental mystery religions or (b) the remains of contemporary or somewhat later Gnostic writings.

(a) In his letter to the Ephesians Ignatius refers to the Eucharist or, more precisely, to "breaking one loaf," and identifies this
loaf as "the medicine of immortality, the antidote for dying,
producing life in Jesus Christ forever." Since, according to Diodorus Siculus, the "medicine of immortality" was given by the
Egyptian goddess Isis to her son Horus, it is assumed that the
term was employed in the Egyptian mysteries and that initiates
were given this medicine. Unfortunately there is no evidence for
this theory, although there is evidence to show that the term
was used metaphorically. In addition, the idea that immortality
was related to the Eucharist is implied in 1 Corinthians 11:30
and clearly stated in the prayers of early Jewish-Christian Didache
(10:3, cf. 9:3; 10.2). Again, the comparison of the Christian life
with a pagan religious procession certainly implies that Ignatius
is acquainted with such processions. It is hard to see, however,
why he should therefore be associated with pagan religions—any
more than he should be associated with engineering because, in
the sentences immediately preceding, he uses metaphors derived
from the construction of a building.

(b) It might be supposed that similarities between Ignatius'
language and that used in writings traditionally ascribed to Paul,
John, and Matthew could be explained by his acquaintance
either with these writings or with the thought of their authors.
Critics of his ideas, however, have been anxious to argue that
though he may have used apostolic writings, he did not think
apostolic thoughts; instead, he interpreted New Testament documents—in so far as he was acquainted with them—in the light
of the Gnostic environment presumably predominant at Antioch.
Before accepting the validity of such an argument we must first
suggest that it is unlikely that anyone, whether Christian or
Gnostic, ancient or modern, actually does or can reproduce the
ideas of earlier writers exactly. A person such as Ignatius, convinced that he is following in the apostles' footsteps, is especially
likely to read himself into their writings. To say this is merely to
say that we must interpret Ignatius (and ourselves) historically.

When we look at what is actually known of his setting at

Antioch or in Asia Minor in the early second century, we certainly find that dualistic Gnostic systems are already in existence, and it can be shown that ingredients of such systems were present among Christians as early as the time when Colossians, if not 1 Corinthians, was written. Ignatius' fanciful imagery about the star of Bethlehem, however, seems to be based not on Gnostic ideas but on meditation derived from the book of Wisdom. When he assures the Trallians that he can understand heavenly matters such as angelic locations and archontic conjunctions, there is no reason for looking beyond astrology—Christian astrology, to be sure—for the sources of his ideas. In the heavens there exists the glory of the angels, along with archons both visible and invisible, as he tells the Smyrnaeans; these beings must believe in the blood of Christ unless they are to be condemned. But Ignatius' occasional references to angelic beings and, more frequently, to "the prince of this age" suggest that he is a Christian influenced by Pauline and Johannine language (and perhaps at one remove by Jewish apocalyptic), not a crypto-Gnostic.

It should be added that the method employed by some scholars in order to show how Gnostic Ignatius was is not altogether correct. Undeniably there are parallels between some of the language of Ignatius and some of the language used in Gnostic writings as early as the middle of the second century; fresh instances have been provided by the Gnostic gospels of Thomas and Philip. These parallels cannot be used, however, to prove that Ignatius was a Gnostic, for the Gnostics involved regarded themselves as Christians, or hyper-Christians, interpreting the true meaning of the Christian tradition. Parallels between what they said and what Ignatius said do not necessarily prove more than that both they and he were interpreting the Christian tradition (1) in rather similar ways, at some points, and (2) quite possibly in similar environments often closer to esoteric Judaism and to Hellenistic religiosity than to the kinds of Judaism (and Christianity) reflected in most of the other Christian literature we possess. Not everything in Gnostic books, as van Unnik has observed, is Gnostic; it is the context that makes it so.[2]

In order to show that Ignatius was chiefly a Christian we must consider various doctrines about which questions have been raised.

[2] W. C. van Unnik, in F. L. Cross, ed., *The Jung Codex* (London, 1955), 101-103.

DOCTRINE OF GOD

Ignatius' emphasis on the unity of God has been criticized by
H. W. Bartsch in his article on him in *Die Religion in Geschichte
und Gegenwart*.[1]

> The idea of the unity of God is not based on the biblical expres-
> sions of the uniqueness of God but on the Gnostic principle of unity
> which combines theology with soteriology. This comprehensive prin-
> ciple was the door through which Gnostic systems and mythical con-
> ceptions entered early Christian literature.

It is undeniable that Ignatius' ideas are not exclusively biblical.
Instead, they are interpretations of biblical doctrines in new circumstances provided by the Graeco-Roman world. The word
henotēs (oneness, unity) occurs in the New Testament only in
Ephesians and Colossians, as Bartsch p. 11 has pointed out; [2] but
these letters are part of the New Testament and Ignatius knew
both of them.

Preiss pp. 221-225, 239-241 has similarly insisted that Ignatius'
ideas about God are close to Gnosticism because there is "no
allusion at all to the idea of creation." In the inscription to the
Romans, God is described as "having willed (*thelēsantos*) all
things that are," but Preiss (following Bauer) claims that the
word means "having loved." (For a defense of the traditional
translation see commentary.) Again, Ignatius speaks of Jesus as
God's Word (Magn. 8:2); but whereas other early Christian
writers associate the Word with creation, Ignatius lays stress on
the novelty of revelation: the Word proceeded from silence. (But
the prophets proclaimed the gospel, Philad. 5:2.) Finally, Ignatius says that before the ages Jesus Christ was with the Father
(no mention of creation) but was made manifest at the end
(Magn. 6:1). The only passage implicitly related to creation is
Eph. 15:1, where Psalm 32:9 LXX ("he spoke, and it happened")
is referred to the "one teacher"—that is, Jesus. Preiss also claims

[1] 3d ed. (Tübingen, 1959), III, 667.
[2] For titles of books cited only by author's name and page number see
the Bibliography.

5

that in Ignatius' view the divine plan (*oikonomia*) began with Jesus; the Old Testament revelation was significant only in so far as it pointed toward him. (This is an argument from silence; the word *oikonomia* occurs only three times, in Eph. 6:1; 18:2; and 20:1, but Ignatius actually insists that there was a divine plan reflected in the Old Testament but perfected in the gospel, Philad. 9:1-2.)

We therefore regard Preiss's claim as an exaggeration. Though Ignatius does refer to words of Psalm 32 to Christ, he presumably referred them to the Father as well, for he held that the Father spoke through Jesus Christ (Rom. 8:2). We should add that Ignatius' ideas were expressed within a context of liturgical worship, and in that worship, especially at the Eucharist, the prayers often included thanksgiving for God's work of creation (Did. 10:3; Justin, *Dialogue* 41; perhaps Theophilus, *Ad Autol.* 1, 6-7 is also liturgical).[3]

We should agree, however, that as in the New Testament writings, God the Father is primarily the Redeemer; no one comes to him but through Jesus (John 14:6). Though Ignatius speaks of the Father's power (Magn. 3:1), grace (Magn. inscr.), and love (Philad. 1:1), he is much more concerned with the Father as the Father of Jesus Christ (Eph. 2:1; Trall. inscr.; Rom. inscr.). Jesus Christ came from the Father and went to the Father (Magn. 7:2; Eph. 5:1; Smyrn. 3:3). He imitated the Father (Philad. 7:2) and now follows him (Smyrn. 8:1); he represents and is the Father's "mouth" (Rom. 8:2) and will (Eph. 3:2). The Father raised him from the dead (Trall. 9:2; Smyrn. 7:1) and he is now in the Father (Rom. 3:3). The Church, like Eden, is the "plantation of the Father" (Trall. 11:1; Philad. 3:1), and Christians sing to the Father through or in Jesus Christ (Eph 4:2; Rom. 2:2), the "door" to the Father (Philad. 9:1).[4]

---

[3] See *Anglican Theological Review* 30 (1948), 91-94.

[4] Most of these ideas are to be found, explicitly or implicitly, in the Gospel of John.

CHRISTOLOGY

The term used of Jesus most frequently is the double name "Jesus Christ" (112 times); occasionally we find "Christ Jesus" (13 times) or "Jesus" (3 times) or "Christ" (4 times). The name Jesus Christ occurs either by itself or in combination with titles such as "Lord," "God," and "Savior."

Jesus is called "God" in neither of the two letters concerned with the Judaizing heresy (Magnesians, Philadelphians), but in the others there are eleven definite examples of this usage.

Eph. inscr.	"Jesus Christ our God"
1:1	"the blood of God"
7:2	"in man, God"
15:3	"our God"
18:2	"our God, Jesus the Christ"
19:3	"God was manifest as man"
Rom. inscr.	"Jesus Christ our God" (twice)
3:3	"our God Jesus Christ"
6:3	"the passion of my God"
Smyrn. 1:1	"Jesus Christ, the God who . . ."
Polyc. 8:3	"our God Jesus Christ"

Four other passages are uncertain as to text or meaning. (1) Ephesians 17:2 contains a reference to "the knowlege of God, i.e., Jesus Christ," but as in Ignatius' model (Col. 2:2), Jesus Christ may be the knowledge of God rather than God. (2) Trallians 7:1 can be translated either "inseparable from the God Jesus Christ" or "inseparable from God, Jesus Christ, and . . . ." Though the former translation seems the more likely, it remains uncertain. (3) The statement about the blood of Christ "that it is of God" (Smyrn. 6:1) is a Monophysite interpolation, inconsistent with what Ignatius is saying. (4) The description of two deacons as "deacons of God Christ" (Smyrn. 10:1) suggests that copyists were unable to decide between "God" (the reading of the fifth-century papyrus and the Armenian version) and "Christ" and therefore combined them. These passages are unimportant, however, as compared with the first eleven.

Ignatius is insisting upon the divine function, and also upon the divine nature, of the incarnate Lord, just as certain New Testament writers also insist upon it (John 1:1; 20:28; Heb. 1:8-9; Tit. 2:13; 2 Pet. 1:1). Similarly, the roughly contemporary author of 2 Clement begins his sermon by urging his readers to "think about Jesus Christ as of God," and Christians in Pontus, according to a rather hostile reporter, sang hymns "to Christ as to a god" (Pliny, *Ep.* 10, 96, 7). Except in circles strongly influenced by Jewish Christianity—exemplified in the Didache, 1 Clement, and Hermas—there was no hesitation about speaking of Christ as God.

What Ignatius means by "God" is not confined to what he could find in the Old Testament or early Christian tradition. God, and Christ as God, is "eternal, invisible, intangible, impassible" (Polyc. 3:2). This is to say that Ignatius, or other Christians shortly before his time, had introduced into their theology some of the conceptions current in Greek philosophical theology. This development necessarily involved their Christology in a considerable measure of paradox—as in Ignatius' own Christological statements (Polyc. 3:2; Eph. 7:2). In Philadelphians 1:2 he describes the bishop as like God in the virtue and perfection of his mind, his immovability and freedom from wrath, and his gentleness. Only the last of these characteristics is close to biblical doctrines.

Something more should be said about several of the names of Jesus which Ignatius uses. Just as in 1 Clement (32:4; 38:1), the name "Christ Jesus" is employed at points where Ignatius is imitating Pauline expressions or has Pauline ideas in mind (Eph. 1:1; 11:1; 12:2; Magn. inscr.; 8:2; 10:3; Trall. 9:2; Rom. 1:1; 2:2; Philad. 10:1; 11:2). The name "Jesus," on the other hand, is not used in Clement's manner. Clement employs it where he is speaking of "the words of the Lord Jesus" (1 Clem. 13:1; 46:7) or of "the Lord Jesus, humanly speaking (*kata sarka*)" (1 Clem. 32:2); Ignatius almost certainly reflects Johannine usage. The three examples are these:

Eph. 15:2   He who has truly acquired the word of Jesus can also hear his silence (cf. John 14:2, 7, 9).
Magn. 1:2   . . . union of (or, with) . . . Jesus and the Father (John 17:11, 21).
Philad. 5:1   . . . fleeing to the gospel as to the flesh of Jesus (cf. John 6:51-58).

Finally, Ignatius apparently reserves the title "Christ" for the risen and exalted Lord. There are four examples:

> Magn. 13:2 The apostles were subject to Christ (avoids repetition of "Jesus Christ").
> Rom. 4:1 . . . that I may be found the pure bread of Christ.
> Rom. 4:2 Beseech Christ on my behalf (only example of prayer *to* Christ).
> Smyrn. 6:1 heavenly beings must believe in the blood of Christ.

This is not to say that he cannot use "Jesus Christ" under such circumstances; it is only that the term "Christ" does not otherwise appear.

Ignatius can also speak of Jesus as the Son (co-ordinate with the Father and the Spirit, Magn. 13:1—perhaps based on Matt. 28:19), the Son of the Father (Rom. inscr.; cf. Magn. 8:2), or Son of man and Son of God (Eph. 20:2). By these last terms Ignatius understands that Jesus was human and divine. As Son of God he was also God's "Word proceeding from silence" (Magn. 8:2—paralleled in later Valentinian thought). He is timeless, invisible (though visible for us), intangible, impassible (though passible for us); he endured in every way for us (Polyc. 3:2; cf. Eph. 7:2).

As Son of man he was a teacher (cf. Corwin pp. 105-106) who gave commandments, a high priest who is the door to the Father (Heb. 2:17, etc.; John 10:7; Philad. 9:1), a physician (Eph. 7:2). He can be called the "new man" (Eph. 20:1) or the "perfect man" (Smyrn. 4:2).

More metaphorically, he is the plan of the Father (Eph. 3:2) or the Father's mouth (Rom. 8:2; cf. Ode of Solomon 12:11; Gospel of Truth pp. 26, 34). He is the knowledge of God (Eph. 17:2). He is joy (Magn. 7:1). He is the new leaven of 1 Cor. 5:7 (Magn. 10:2). He is the common hope of Christians (Eph. 21:2; Magn. 11:1; Trall. inscr.; Philad. 11:2; cf. Philad. 5:2; 1 Tim. 1:1: "Christ Jesus our hope," with Tit. 1:4, "common faith").

His relation to the Old Testament is discussed primarily in the two letters about Judaism. There we read that the Old Testament prophets pointed toward his coming (Philad. 9:2) and were inspired by his grace (Magn. 8:2). When he came, he raised them from the dead (Magn. 9:2), and patriarchs and prophets alike now approach the Father through him (Philad. 9:1).

There are three passages in Ignatius' letters which can be called credal, not in the sense that they necessarily reflect anything being used as a formula at Antioch but in the sense that they sum up matters which then and later were important for the defining of Christian belief. (1) Ephesians 18:2: "our God, Jesus the Christ, was conceived by Mary in accordance with the plan of God—of the seed of David and of the Holy Spirit; he was born and was baptized to purify the water by the passion." (2) Trallians 9:1-2: "Jesus Christ, who was of the family of David, who was of Mary, who was truly born, ate and drank, was truly persecuted under Pontius Pilate, was truly crucified and died, while heavenly, earthly, and subterranean beings looked on. He was also truly raised from the dead. . . ." (3) Smyrnaeans 1:1-2: "he is truly of the family of David as to the flesh, Son of God by God's will and power, truly born of a virgin, baptized by John so that all righteousness might be fulfilled by him, truly nailed for us in the flesh under Pontius Pilate and the tetrarch Herod. . . ."

These passages are clearly based on New Testament ideas and language. References to the seed of David and to the Holy Spirit come from Romans 1:3-4; mention of Mary, from the Gospels of Matthew and Luke or the traditions underlying them. The "fulfilment of all righteousness" can come only from Matthew 3:15, while the tradition that Jesus was nailed to the cross is Johannine—and anti-Docetic (John 20:25).

The essential purpose of the work or plan of God in Christ is set forth in the "mythical" passage in Ephesians 19. Magic was dissolved; every bond of wickedness vanished; ignorance was abolished; and the "old kingdom" (of Satan) was destroyed. God, manifest as man, brought the newness of eternal life, and God's plan took its beginning. It was to result in the abolition of death.

Death was abolished indeed on the first Lord's Day, when our life sprang up through the Lord and his death (Magn. 9:1). Ignatius does not explain this point fully; evidently he relies on Pauline and Johannine antecedents. There is nothing mechanical about life after death, however. It depends upon imitation, at least for Ignatius, who is giving himself to death (Smyrn. 4:2).

For this reason the passion or suffering of Christ is intensely important for Ignatius. Through the passion of Christ comes election (Eph. inscr.), the call to be members of him (Trall. 11:2). His passion is our resurrection (Smyrn. 5:3); Ignatius

often mentions passion and resurrection together. Put more fully, this means that Christ suffered for us so that we might be saved (Smyrn. 2:1) or "the flesh of Jesus Christ suffered for our sins" (7:1). Obviously, if Christ did not really suffer, men could receive no real benefits from his passion. This is why Ignatius is so militantly opposed to Docetism, the heresy which viewed Christ's life and sufferings as "semblance." Because of Ignatius' view of the *imitatio Christi,* the Christian attains to resurrection through his own suffering as well as that of Christ (Rom. 4:3; 6:3; Polyc. 7:1). Indeed, he is "nailed to the cross of the Lord Jesus Christ" (Smyrn. 1:1, a vivid reminiscence of Paul's words about being crucified with Christ, Gal. 2:20). He dies into his passion (Magn. 5:2), partakes of his passion (Philad. 3:3), is raised in him (Trall. 9:2) and joined to him (Eph. 5:1)—because he imitates the passion of his God (Rom. 6:3; for these passages cf. Richardson pp. 65-66).

The key word here is "imitation," which Ignatius almost certainly derived from the Pauline epistles (1 Cor. 4:16; 11:1; Gal. 4:12; Phil. 3:17; 1 Thess. 1:6; 2:14; 2 Thess. 3:7, 9—and especially Eph. 5:1: "be imitators of God," a phrase repeated by Ignatius in Eph. 1:1 and Trall. 1:2). Christians should imitate the Lord (Eph. 10:3) and, specifically, the passion of their God (Rom. 6:3). The pattern of imitation is theologically grounded in the imitation of the Father by Jesus Christ (Philad. 7:2). Here Ignatius' statement reflects two sources. First, in form it resembles Paul's counsel to the Corinthians to imitate him as he imitates Christ (1 Cor. 11:1). Second, the Son's imitation of the Father is a point emphasized in the gospel of John (5:19, "whatever he may do, the Son does likewise"). The two kinds of expression are easily reconcilable, for on Paul's grounds there is a hierarchical structure of man-Christ-God (1 Cor. 3:23; 11:3). As the apostle imitates Christ, so Christ imitates God.

To imitate someone means to be or to become his disciple. But Ignatius cannot speak of himself or of others as fully disciples of Jesus Christ, for they have not fully imitated him; they have not experienced the passion. The Old Testament prophets were disciples of Jesus Christ in the Spirit (Magn. 9:2), for they were persecuted (Magn. 8:2). But after their times there have been no disciples in the true sense, except for the apostles (whom Ignatius does not call disciples). He himself is not a disciple

(Trall. 5:2), though he is beginning to be one (Eph. 3:1; Rom. 3:2; 5:3). He hopes to be found the disciple of the Smyrnaeans at the resurrection (Polyc. 7:1).

What becoming a disciple finally means is "attaining to God," a phrase which Ignatius frequently uses. This means to "reach God," but we cannot neglect the variety of the ways in which Ignatius depicts the goal and the means to the goal. He does not always speak of "attaining to God"; twice he speaks of attaining to Jesus Christ (Rom. 5:3), once of attaining to the destined lot (of martyrdom, Rom. 1:2), and once of making secure the lot in which God's mercy had placed him (Philad. 5:1; cf. Trall. 12:3). He will attain through suffering (Polyc. 7:1) and through the wild beasts (Eph. 1:2; Rom. 4:1), but especially through the prayers of the churches (Magn. 14:1; Rom. 8:3; Smyrn. 11:1). If he can go on this course he will be following in Paul's footsteps (Eph. 12:2).

This "triumph through suffering" will belong not to Ignatius alone but to other Christians as well. He tells the Smyrnaeans that they will attain to God, their "reward," if they endure everything for him (Smyrn. 9:2), just as Ignatius himself is doing (Smyrn. 4:2). Not only Ignatius but all Christians as well will be found to be disciples of Jesus Christ if they endure (Magn. 9:1; Polyc. 2:3).

MARTYRDOM

It is undeniable that Ignatius desires to be a martyr. He asks the Roman Christians not to hinder his being eaten by the wild beasts in the arena. He insists that he is dying "willingly" (Rom. 4:1). Many critics have found his attitude unpalatable; Preiss (pp. 199-202) compares Ignatius with Paul as reflected in Philippians, to the disadvantage of the former. But it might be observed that Ignatius' voluntary dying is not unlike Paul's voluntary apostleship (1 Cor. 9:17). If Paul preaches "willingly," he receives a reward; and Ignatius is no more averse to a reward than Paul is. As for his whole emphasis on martyrdom, it is hard to believe that he has not read the great Pauline text in Colossians 1:24-29.

> Now I rejoice in my sufferings on your behalf, and I fill up what is lacking in the tribulations of Christ in my flesh on behalf of his body, which is the Church, of which I became a minister in accordance with the plan of God which was given me, to fill full the word of God for you, the mystery which was hidden from the ages and the generations, but now has been made manifest to his saints, for whom God willed to make known what is the richness of the glory of this mystery among the gentiles—Christ in you, the hope of glory. We proclaim him by instructing every man and teaching every man in all wisdom, so that we may present every man perfect in Christ. For this I toil, struggling in accordance with the energy at work in me with power.

Paul's words point toward Ignatius' idea of his own role. To be sure, Paul's ideas do not seem to be especially "mystical," whereas Ignatius often speaks of "attaining to God"; but apart from this point the resemblance is striking. As Hanson [1] points out, the apostle's suffering, like Christ's, is for the Church; what Christ achieved in principle is now made actual and is realized. Paul is Christ's apostle and represents him; "as a logical consequence of this it follows that he must suffer in the same way as

[1] S. Hanson, *The Unity of the Church in the New Testament: Colossians and Ephesians* (Uppsala, 1946), 119-121.

14THE APOSTOLIC FATHERS

the Sender suffered." The strict logic of this sentence is not altogether obvious, but it might well have seemed obvious to Ignatius.

In our view, indeed, Ignatius' conception of his own work is practically identical with Paul's conception of his own as interpreted by Hans Windisch (and summarized by E. Beijer [2]):

> His sufferings are Christ's sufferings. For Paul suffering is a sacrament through which the sharing of his life with Christ comes to be realized. In this way his sufferings too acquire the power of vicarious sacrifice. The classical expression of this . . . is in Colossians 1:24.

The expression Windisch used of Paul was *simul sanctus et nondum perfectus;* [3] and this admirably summarized Ignatius' ideas.

Ignatius employs several expressions to designate his own sacrifice. The word *peripsēma* (Eph. 8:1; 18:1) might mean no more than "offscouring" (1 Cor. 4:13) were it not that in the first passage Ignatius also says "I am . . . consecrated for you." He also refers to himself explicitly as an *antipsychon,* or "ransom" (Eph. 21:1; Smyrn. 10:2; Polyc. 2:3; 6:1), a term also used in the contemporary, perhaps Antiochene 4 Maccabees (6:29; 17:21). Most important are his statements in Romans, where he depicts himself as a sacrificial libation poured out to God (Rom. 2:2; cf. Phil. 2:17; 2 Tim. 4:6) and as a sacrifice (Rom. 4:2; cf. Phil. 2:17; Rom. 12:1).[4]

Indeed, while the word *thysiastērion* usually means "sanctuary" (though the sanctuary is a place of sacrifice) in his letters, he once uses it of the "altar" on which he is to be poured out (Rom. 2:2).

A question constantly in Ignatius' mind is that of being worthy (*axios*). On the one hand, Jesus' work was worthy of the Father (Eph. 15:1); churches, ministers, and martyrs can be called worthy of God or of their tasks (9 examples). Ignatius is very fond of using words compounded with *axios* in the same way (17 examples). He himself has been judged worthy to bear the name "Theophorus" (Magn. inscr.; 1:2). On the other hand, he feels a distinct sense of unworthiness. Not only does he pray,

[2] *Zeitschrift für die neutestamentliche Wissenschaft* 48 (1957), 35.
[3] *Ibid.,* n. 49; Windisch, *Paulus und Christus* (Leipzig, 1934), 271; cf. 307-308.
[4] It may be significant that he does not use this language in writing to churches where schism and heresy are especially prominent—Magnesians, Trallians, Philadelphians.

"May I have joy, if I be worthy" (Eph. 2:2; Magn. 12:1, perhaps imitating Paul's language in Philemon 20), but he clearly states that he is unworthy to be called a member of the Syrian church (Magn. 14:1; Trall. 13:1; Rom. 9:2; Smyrn. 11:1). This unworthiness is partly derivative, being based on 1 Corinthians 15:8-10; but the use of Pauline language does not mean that Ignatius fails to share Paul's attitude. The genuineness of Ignatius' humility is attested by what he says in Trallians 4:2: "I desire to suffer, but I do not know if I am worthy." Those who suffer are already worthy of God (Rom. 10:2) and become worthy by God's grace (Smyrn. 11:1). Thus suffering produces worthiness, either actually or proleptically.

Once more, Ignatius' ideas are not very different from those found in the New Testament. The disciple who is like his Lord takes up his cross and follows him (Mark 8:34-35 and parallels); when Paul describes his own "achievements" for the gospel, he provides lists of the sufferings he has undergone (I Cor. 4:9-13; 2 Cor. 4:7-10; 6:4-10; 11:23-27). The apostle shares in Christ's sufferings and is conformed to his death so that somehow he may attain to the resurrection (Phil. 3:10-14).

FAITH AND ESCHATOLOGY

It might appear that Ignatius has minimized the function of faith and has instead insisted upon works, specifically the "work" of martyrdom. But (1) the sharp differentiation of faith from works arose in the Pauline epistles primarily because Paul was dealing with those who insisted upon the importance of keeping all or part of the Jewish law; it was not necessarily relevant under all other circumstances; [1] and (2) we must examine what Ignatius actually says about faith. On the one hand, faith is the beginning of the Christian life as love is its goal (Eph. 14:1); nothing is preferable to the union of faith with love (Magn. 1:1), for in this union the Christian "prospers" (Magn. 13:1). The faith and love of the Ephesian church gave it its reputation (Eph 1:1). Obviously Ignatius views faith as somehow co-ordinate with works, for in his military image he begins with baptism, continues with faith, love, and endurance, and ends with works (Polyc. 6:2). On the other hand, faith is directed toward Jesus Christ (Magn. 1:1), though it is also "through" him (Philad. 8:2), and he himself was crucified for his faith in God (Eph. 16:2; cf. the ambiguous Eph. 20:1). Ignatius can say, "We who believe in Christ Jesus" (Trall. 9:2) or "I know and believe" (Smyrn. 3:1; cf. Paul, Rom. 14:14). He can refer to "immovable faith" (Smyrn. 1:1) or the harmony of faith (Eph. 13:1; cf. Philad. 11:2: faith, love, and harmony); he can speak of being firm in the faith (Eph. 10:2; cf. Col. 1:23) or of holding the faith in love (Philad. 9:2). Specifically, he says that by believing in the death of Jesus Christ one can escape from dying (Trall. 2:1) or that by believing in the blood of Christ one can escape judgment (Smyrn. 6:1). Ignatius expresses his thought about faith most vividly when he writes, "I have confidence in grace, that you are ready to do the good deed appropriate to God" (Polyc. 7:3) and "I believe in the grace of Jesus Christ, and he will loose every bond from you"

[1] K. Stendahl, "The Apostle Paul and the Introspective Conscience of the West," *Harvard Theological Review* 56 (1963), 199-215.

(Philad. 8:1). The first passage simply means that Ignatius has faith in the divine grace which makes men ready for good works (cf. Paul, Eph. 2:8-10). The second occurs just after Ignatius has mentioned repentance and forgiveness and seems to imply that God forgives because of his gift of grace in Christ.

This faith is not explicitly related to justification, an idea which—since Ignatius is not concerned with the problem of the Jewish law—is almost absent from his writings. By being baptized, Jesus fulfilled or accomplished all righteousness (Smyrn. 1:1; Matt. 3:15). Ignatius can speak of the "just nature" of the Ephesians (1:1). But he is aware of the ambiguous character of righteousness: "the righteous man is his own accuser," he writes, quoting Proverbs 18:17 (Magn. 12:1), and he himself hopes to be justified by the Philadelphians' prayer (8:2). "I become more a disciple because of their [his guards'] injustices, but 'not by this am I justified'" (Rom. 5:1, an allusion to 1 Cor. 4:4; see Torrance p. 67). He will be made righteous, or justified, only through his sacrificial death. It must be said, however, that faith in Jesus' death results in eternal life (Trall. 2:1), and that since it is the beginning of the Christian life it is obviously indispensable.

Ignatius says little about sin or sinning, and never refers to sinners. When he says that the flesh of Jesus "suffered for our sins" (Smyrn. 7:1), he is doubtless thinking of sins committed before baptism (cf. Eph. 18:2). His statement that "no one who professes faith sins" (Eph. 14:2) recalls 1 John 3:6: "Everyone who remains in him does not sin." Postbaptismal sin can be forgiven, however, if sinners repent and come to the unity of God and the Church (Philad. 3:2, 8:1, Smyrn. 9:1); power to repent will be given them by Jesus Christ (Smyrn. 4:1; cf. 5:3); indeed, "the hope of repentance" is already in them (Eph. 10:1).

It has been claimed that Ignatius has no place for eschatology in his thought. In so far as eschatology is identified with Jewish apocalyptic eschatology, this claim is generally correct, although in Ephesians 11:1 he states that "these are the last times" (cf. 1 John 2:18) and urges his readers either to fear the wrath to come or to love the grace which is present. This appeal resembles the Pauline summary about "Jesus who delivers us from the wrath to come" (1 Thess. 1:10; cf. Rom. 5:9). But Ignatius mentions divine wrath only here and speaks of judgment only in this passage

and in Smyrnaeans 6:1. We note, however, that his insistence upon grace as present is close to Paul's Ephesians (2:5-8): "by grace you have been saved." No more than Paul (Phil. 1:19-26) does he insist upon general eschatological notions as he confronts his own death. Christ has already come "at the end" (Magn. 6:1), though Christians await his coming (Polyc. 3:2). Now is the occasion for Christians to repent fully (Smyrn. 9:1) or to perform what God has called them to do (Rom. 2:1, Polyc. 2:3).

SPIRIT AND FLESH

Ignatius never uses the word "spirit" in the plural. Sometimes he speaks explicitly of the Holy Spirit (Eph. 9:1; 18:2; Philad. inscr.; cf. Smyrn. 13:1) or of Son, Father, and Spirit (Magn. 13:1). He can speak of the united flesh and spirit of Jesus Christ (Magn. 1:2; Smyrn. 3:2) or of Jesus as an "undivided spirit" (Magn. 15:1). Often flesh and spirit represent the totality of human nature (6 instances), but the spirit, originating in God, is superior to the flesh because of the knowledge it conveys (Philad. 7:1-2). In the spirit (or, in spirit) the prophets were disciples of Jesus (Magn. 9:2). The spirit of man must keep awake (Polyc. 1:3); Ignatius uses the phrase "my spirit" when he speaks of his most personal goals (Eph. 18:1; Trall. 12:1; Rom. 9:3; Smyrn. 10:2). He once mentions a triad of flesh, soul, and spirit (Philad. 11:2), apparently alluding to 1 Thessalonians 5:23, where Paul referred to spirit, soul, and body. The word "spiritual" usually occurs with "fleshly" or "carnal."

Generally speaking, Ignatius uses "flesh" where Paul would have used "body" (see on Philad. 4:1) and thus is closer to John. He uses the word "body" four times, thrice in reference to his own body (Rom. 4:2; 5:3), once to the body of Christ's Church (Smyrn. 1:2). The word *sōmateion*, related to it, occurs in Smyrn. 11:2 (see commentary). "Soul" appears only twice, once of "my soul" (Philad. 1:2, where we might expect "my spirit") and once in the triad we have already mentioned.

"Flesh" is often associated with "spirit," as we have said, but it needs to be controlled by God or the Christian (cf. Philad. 7:2). The most striking feature of Ignatius' use of "flesh" is in relation to the Eucharist (Rom. 7:3; Philad. 4:1; Smyrn. 7:1). But this flesh is not "mere" flesh; with the flesh of Jesus, Ignatius identifies the bread of God (Rom. 7:3) and faith (Trall. 8:1) and parallels the gospel (Philad. 5:1), and he identifies Jesus' blood as joy (Philad. inscr.) or love (Rom. 7:3; Trall. 8:1) or relates it to love (Smyrn. 1:1; cf. Paul, Rom. 5:9).

CHURCH AND MINISTRY

Christians are those who can be exhorted to live in harmony with God's purpose and recognize that Jesus Christ expresses the Father's purpose while the bishops, appointed throughout the world, express the purpose of Jesus Christ (Eph. 3:2; cf. Philad. inscr.). Christians who live in unity demonstrate that they are "members" of God's Son (Eph. 4:2) in the one body of his Church (Smyrn. 1:2). They are members of Christ, the Head which cannot come to birth apart from the members of the body (Trall. 11:2). They are branches of the cross (Trall. 11:2), which Ignatius identifies with the tree of life in Eden. The Church is like a bride and is loved by the Lord (Polyc. 5:1). It is the church of God, and the various congregations are churches of God (Trall. 2:3; 12:1).

Most of these images of the church are based on Pauline expressions—except for the statement that the ministry of bishops, presbyters, and deacons is essential and necessary. This statement (Trall. 3:1) is paraphrased thus by Lightfoot (p. 159): "Without these three orders no church has a title to the name." Every Ignatian letter except Romans contains sections urging obedience to the bishop. On what grounds can this obedience be recommended?

In Ignatius' view the bishop is analogous to God (Magn. 6:1) or the grace of God (Magn. 2:1), to the Father (Magn. 3:1, Trall. 3:1; Smyrn. 8:1), to the Lord (Eph. 6:1), to Jesus Christ (Trall. 2:1), and to "the commandment" (presumably that of God, Trall. 13:2). The presbytery is parallel to the apostles (Magn. 6:1; Trall. 2:2; 3:1; Philad. 5:1; Smyrn. 8:1) or to the law of Jesus Christ (Magn. 6:1; Trall. 3:1) or a commandment of God (Smyrn. 8:1).

The most common analogies are therefore those drawn between the bishop and God the Father, the deacons and Jesus Christ, and the presbyters and the apostles. This sequence is rather strange. We should not expect the presbyters to be inferior

(in regard to the analogy) to the deacons. It would appear that the bishop and the deacons reflect one strand of development, the presbyters another.

Before we draw too sharp a line between the various orders, however, we should note that all the ministers are viewed as apostolic. According to Eph. 6:1 the bishop, who has been sent by the Lord, is analogous to the apostle (cf. John 13:20; Matt. 10:40). The bishop of Philadelphia obtained his ministry "not from himself or through men" (Philad. 1:1) and in this way resembled the apostle Paul (Gal. 1:1). The presbyters, of course, are apostolic for they occupy the place of the council of the apostles (Magn. 6:1) or the council of God and the college of the apostles (Trall. 3:1). The deacons, as described in Trall. 2:3, are clearly like Paul. As deacons of the mysteries of Jesus Christ (1 Cor. 4:1), they must please all men in every way (1 Cor. 10:33). They are not ministers of food and drink (since the kingdom of God is not eating and drinking, Paul, Rom. 14:17) but servants (1 Cor. 4:1) of the church of God (1 Cor. 10:32). These allusions show that the pattern for their behavior is Pauline.

It is interesting to notice, then, that while the presbyters are explicitly called apostolic, they are not described in terms reminiscent of the apostle Paul; and, on the other hand, the bishops and deacons, not called apostolic, are described in Pauline language.

Apparently the ministry as Ignatius describes it is based on two sources: the "bishops and deacons" of some, if not all, Pauline churches (Paul, Phil. 1:1), and the "presbyters" more characteristically Jewish-Christian. What this means as far as the ministry of the early church as a whole is concerned has been discussed in Volume 1 (pp. 160-173).

THE HERESIES AND THE SOURCES OF
IGNATIUS' IDEAS

It is not clear that every letter of Ignatius is directed against a specific type of heresy. In Romans there is no reference to any; in Ephesians there are references but they are rather vague, as in the letter to Polycarp. On the other hand, Magnesians and Philadelphians are clearly written against Judaizers; Trallians and Smyrnaeans against Docetists.

The Judaizers insist upon the primacy of the Old Testament (Philad. 8:2), especially the prophets (Magn. 8:2; 9:3; Philad. 5:2; 9:1-2) but also, perhaps, apocalyptic or rabbinic traditions (Magn. 8:1). They, or at least some of them, do not seem to be Jews (Philad. 6:1), but they may have claimed that Christianity was based on Judaism (Magn. 10:3).They may keep the Sabbath (Magn. 9:1) and celebrate a Eucharist of their own (Philad. 4:1).

The Docetists are enthusiastic about esoteric spirituality (Trall. 5:1-2; Smyrn. 6:1) and deny the carnal reality of the birth, life, death, and resurrection of Jesus (Trall. 9-10; Smyrn. 1-5). They neglect almsgiving, Eucharist, and prayer (Smyrn. 6-7), like the Gnostics who used the Gospel of Thomas. They may well have rejected the Old Testament (Smyrn. 5:1).

Ignatius therefore had to conduct a two-front war. While attacking one kind of heresy, he had to beware of the other. This situation explains the extent to which his remarks often have been taken to show that there was one heresy, both Docetic and Judaistic. Furthermore, since both groups of opponents regarded themselves as Christians, there were elements in their thought which Ignatius shared.

Daniélou pp. 49-53 has drawn attention to the Jewish Christian elements in Ignatius' thought, and though they are not especially conspicuous they deserve attention. Three terms also occur in Jewish Christian writings: (1) "the name of God" (Eph. 1:3); (2) "the beloved" as a title for Jesus (Smyrn. inscr.); and (3) "plantation" as a name for the Church (Philad. 3:1; cf. Trall.

11:1). In addition, there are such items as the raising of the Old Testament prophets (Magn. 9:2) and the story of the star in Ephesians 19.

These points, and others which Daniélou mentions, show that in spite of Ignatius' opposition to Judaizers there was more in common between him and them than he realized. Presumably the common elements came to him from the orthodox Christian tradition at Antioch, strongly influenced by Judaism.

It is often supposed that Ignatius was strongly influenced by Gnostic ideas, by which he was unconsciously converted to an early form of Gnostic Christianity. The most important evidence in support of this view is provided in Irenaeus' account of the views of Menander, a Samaritan who probably lived in the late first century, and Saturninus, who taught in Syria early in the second century and therefore was approximately a contemporary of Ignatius. The two systems are quite different in their ideas of salvation, even though both are Gnostic.

Menander regarded himself as the savior who had been sent down to the world in order to defeat the angels who made it and to provide immediate resurrection, along with immortality on earth, by means of baptism "into him." Obviously his system was not Christian, although his doctrine of baptism resembles Pauline teaching (especially Col. 3:1; contrast 2 Tim. 2:18) about resurrection as its consequence, as well as Ignatius' language about the Eucharist (Eph. 20:2). It is possible, however, that Menander's language, like that of Ignatius, has been taken too literally by hostile critics.

Saturninus, on the other hand, was not a savior but relied on Gnostic exegesis of Genesis for his picture of the creation of the world and man, and on Gnostic interpretation of the Christian tradition for his picture of the work of the Savior—who "appeared as a man in semblance," and therefore was not born, crucified, or raised from the dead. The Savior was opposed to the God of the Jews and to the other angels who made the world; he came to save those who believed him and have the "spark of life" (given by the unknown Father above) in themselves.

It may be that some of the Docetists whom Ignatius opposed were infected by ideas like those of Saturninus, but there is nothing in his statements about them that would suggest that such is the case. Ignatius may not have wished to discuss their

systematic thought, but from his silence we cannot infer that
it existed. There was "garden-variety" Docetism in the Graeco-
Roman world.[1]

Ignatius' own theological language points in the direction not
of Gnosticism but of vivid imagination expressing itself in equally
vivid rhetoric. Both Perler and Riesenfeld have rightly laid
strong emphasis on the nature of Ignatius' vocabulary and style
rather than upon occasional parallels with later Christian Gnostic
documents.[2] On the other hand, Daniélou's suggestion that Ignatius, like other Apostolic Fathers, is close to Jewish Christianity
is hard to maintain; his affinities seem to lie with Hellenistic
Judaism and Hellenistic Christianity, although in some important aspects, of course, both of these movements were Jewish in
origin.[3]

It is significant that Ignatius never refers to the apostle
John (the "John" of Smyrn. 1:1 is the Baptist) but praises the
Ephesians as "fellow initiates with Paul" (Eph. 12:2) and to the
Romans contrasts himself with Peter and Paul (Rom. 4:3).
This difference accurately reflects the relative importance of
Pauline and Johannine ideas for him. At certain key points he
employs language and ideas derived either from the Gospel of
John or from Johannine circles (e.g. Eph. 2:2; Magn. 7:1; 8:2;
9:1; Rom. 7:3; Smyrn. 7:1), but the influence of Paul's words
and thoughts on him is both more widespread and more thorough-
going. He knows 1 Corinthians practically by heart, but reminis-
cences of most of the other Pauline epistles are very frequent in
his letters. Indeed, it would appear that much of his theological
interpretation of the meaning of his martyrdom is due to his
identification of himself with Paul—in whose footsteps he hopes
to be found.

[1] R. L. P. Milburn in *Journal of Theological Studies* 46 (1945), 68-69.
[2] O. Perler in *Rivista di archeologia cristiana* 25 (1949), 47-72; H. Riesenfeld in *Texte und Untersuchungen* 79 (1961), 312-322.
[3] R. M. Grant, in E. Castelli, ed., *Ermeneutica e tradizione* (Rome,
1963), 198-201.

CRITICISM OF IGNATIUS

Some of the criticisms of Ignatius have already been discussed; some more serious ones remain. It is undeniable that this bishop of Antioch has an exalted idea of his own office and of himself as following in the footsteps of Christ and the apostles. One might say that he imitates Paul as Paul imitates Christ, who in turn imitates the Father. Obviously he would not have said that he was not giving commands in apostolic fashion had he not envisaged the possibility of doing so (Trall. 3:3; Rom. 4:3). The Pauline epistle he knows best is just the one in which Paul is most insistent upon his apostolic authority. And just as in that epistle, 1 Corinthians, Paul constantly claims to be right as against his Corinthian converts,[1] so Ignatius incessantly argues that his opponents are totally wrong. His approach may be described as *fortiter in modo, fortiter in re*. From his letters it is hard to see how his opponents can have regarded themselves as Christians—and yet they did so.

In his theology the Spirit plays a minor role. To use later language, for him the Trinity consists primarily of two persons, the Father and the Son; in Magnesians 13:1 the Spirit is almost an afterthought. The Spirit speaks to the churches (as in Rev. 2:7, etc.), but the voice of the Spirit, "God's own voice" (Philad. 7:1-2) is expressed only through the bishop—Ignatius. As we have seen, after Torrance, there is not much emphasis on grace and there is none on charismatic gifts or the diversity of such gifts.

This is to say that while Ignatius' ideas are not unorthodox, they are (1) exaggerated in the direction of authoritarianism and (2) deficient in regard to the Holy Spirit and its activities. He provides us with an example of an impassioned Christian bishop-martyr but not with a model for Christian life in its potential totality.

[1] On this point see J. C. Hurd, Jr., *The Origin of I Corinthians* (London–New York, 1965).

EPHESIANS

OUTLINE

Salutation
A. Ignatius' gratitude for the visit of Onesimus and others (1:1–2:2)
B. Exhortation to the Ephesians (3:1-2)
C. Unity with the Bishop (4:1–6:1)
D. The orthodoxy of the Ephesians (6:2–10:2)
E. Eschatological exhortations (11:1–13:2)
F. The consequences of faith and love (14:1–16:2)
G. God's plan in the work and life of Jesus (17:1–20:2)
H. Final greeting (21:1-2)

Ephesians

Salutation

Ignatius, also called Theophorus, to the church constituted at Ephesus in Asia—blessed in greatness by the fullness of God the Father, foreordained before the ages to be in lasting and unchanging glory forever, united and elect in genuine suffering (by the will of the Father and Jesus Christ our God), most worthy of blessing: abundant greeting in Jesus Christ and in blameless joy.

Salutation. The salutations of Ignatius' letters follow a remarkably fixed pattern. All of them begin with his name, which he sets forth as "Ignatius who is also God-bearer," and in the simplest salutation (the letter to Polycarp) he next mentions the recipient and his office; finally he says "abundant greeting." The letters to churches contain brief descriptions of their state of having been blessed (Ephesians, Magnesians) or being beloved (Trallians) or, most commonly, having received mercy (Romans, Philadelphians, Smyrnaeans). The divine source of this condition is next mentioned, and the nature of the divine gifts is often further developed. If the circumstances require—especially in Romans—the spiritual greatness of the church is set forth at length. At the end come the specific words of salutation: "abundant greeting" (except in Philadelphians), thrice accompanied (Ephesians, Romans, Smyrnaeans) by the word "blameless."

These salutations are in part based upon passages found in the Pauline epistles. Thus the one addressed to the Ephesians is partly derived from the Pauline Ephesians 1:3-14 (actually a doxology), while that addressed to the Smyrnaeans is partly derived from 1 Corinthians 1:4-7 (part of a thanksgiving). This is to say that Ignatius has combined the Pauline salutation and thanksgiving in his own salutation. He himself says that he is greeting the Trallians "in apostolic fashion" —and the salutation of Trallians contains echoes of Colossians 1:19-20, 27.

Just as Paul often uses his thanksgivings to indicate what he is going to discuss in the body of his letters, so Ignatius sets the tone in his salutations for the letters that follow. Two special points deserve mention. The salutation to Polycarp is unusually brief because Ignatius has already praised the church of Smyrna in another salutation. And the words "abundant greeting" are absent from Philadelphians probably because Ignatius cannot bring himself to the pitch of cordiality which their presence would suggest.

A. Ignatius' gratitude for the visit of
Onesimus and others (1:1–2:2)

1 I became acquainted through God with your well-beloved name which you acquired because of your righteous nature in

---

It should also be noted that in none of the salutations does Ignatius refer to himself as a bishop, whereas Paul usually referred to himself as an apostle. Ignatius is no apostle (Trall. 3:3; Rom. 4:3); he speaks of himself only once as a bishop (Rom. 2:2) and four times calls deacons "fellow slaves" (Eph. 2:1; Magn. 2:1; Philad. 4:1; Smyrn. 12:2). His authority in relation to the churches and persons to whom he writes is not episcopal but personal; he is beginning to be a disciple and speaks as to fellow pupils (Eph. 3:1).

His name, originally Latin (Egnatius), had become Greek by the time in which he wrote. While he uses occasional Latin words, notably in Polyc. 6:2, he is not necessarily a Roman; his Greek is typical of Asian rhetoric (see H. Riesenfeld in *Texte und Untersuchungen* 79 [1961], 312-322). He also has the name Theophorus or "God-bearer," which he uses as an adjective to describe Christians in Ephesians 9:2. He may have received it as a "Christian name" at baptism, though this is uncertain (see Bauer p. 191).

The terms used of the Ephesian church, as Lightfoot p. 23 noted, are strikingly reminiscent of Paul's Ephesians, and we may well suppose that by Ignatius' time that letter had been regarded as addressed to Ephesus. Lightfoot points out that Clement, writing to the Corinthians, uses 1 Corinthians, just as Polycarp, writing to the Philippians, uses Philippians. The church is blessed by the "will" or "purpose" of God (Rom. inscr.), as are its ministry (Philad. inscr.) and the actions of the bishops (Trall. 1:1; Smyrn. 11:1; Polyc. 8:1); Christ was God's Son by God's will (Smyrn. 1:1). See on Ephesians 3:2.

Ignatius sends the Ephesians "abundant greeting in Jesus Christ and in blameless joy." As Bauer p. 195 points out, "abundant greeting" is a phrase characteristic of Hellenistic letters; Ignatius himself was fond of it, as it occurs in all his letters except Philadelphians, three times (Ephesians, Magnesians, Romans) with the "Christianizing" phrase "in Jesus Christ." Similarly, "blameless joy" is mentioned again in Magnesians 7:1, and "blameless" is found in Trallians 1:1; 13:3 (the beginning and the end of the letter) and elsewhere (Rom. inscr.; Smyrn. inscr.; Polyc. 1:1; see on Eph. 4:2). It is Ignatius' hope that their joy may not be accompanied by blame for anything; "perfect joy" would be synonymous, and actually he identifies "blameless joy" as "Jesus Christ" in Magnesians 7:1. (Paul too uses "blameless" of Christians: Phil. 2:15; Col. 1:22; Eph. 1:4; 5:27.) For Ignatius, however, Jesus Christ is more than "blameless joy"; he is "our God" (see Introduction).

1:1–3. The form which Ignatius follows here is also employed in

relation to faith and love in Christ Jesus our Savior. You are imitators of God, and after rekindling, by the blood of God, the task natural to you, you have completed it perfectly. 2. For when you heard that I had been sent in bonds from Syria for our common name and hope, and was hoping by your prayer to attain to fighting wild beasts at Rome—so that by thus attaining I might be able to be a disciple—you hastened to see me. 3. Since, then, I received your whole congregation in God's name in the person of Onesimus, a man of inexpressible love and (humanly speaking) your bishop, I beseech you by Jesus Christ to love him and, all of you, to be like him. For blessed is he who gave you the gift, worthy as you are, of obtaining such a bishop.

Trallians 1:1 and Polycarp 1:1, as W. R. Schoedel has pointed out (*Journal of Theological Studies* 15 [1964], 309-310). First comes a description of what he has "welcomed," then (usually) a verb to indicate his doxology-response, and finally some words about his readers. The "name" of the Ephesians is probably related to *ephesis* not only as meaning "longed for" or "desired" (Bauer p. 196) but also, and especially, as meaning "mission" or "sending" (Schoedel). Therefore he can say that they have obtained their name by their "just nature"; they "spontaneously ('naturally') behave in a just and righteous manner" (Schoedel). The "name" is therefore not that of the bishop Onesimus, and no inferences can be drawn from this passage to suggest that he is the slave of Paul's letter to Philemon (against J. Knox, *Philemon Among the Letters of Paul* [Chicago, 1935], 54-56). Ignatius very rarely uses the word "just" or "righteous"; indeed, it occurs elsewhere only in Magnesians 12:1, a quotation from Proverbs 18:17. He proceeds immediately to mention faith and love, and probably because he associates them with Paul's ideas he employs the Pauline appellation "Christ Jesus" (other examples are also related to Paul). For Christ Jesus as Savior compare Titus 1:4; 2:13; in the latter passage he is also called "God," and similarly, Ignatius proceeds to speak of imitating God (cf. Philad. 7:2). His words are reminiscent of Paul's Ephesians 5:1-2: "Become imitators of God as beloved children and walk in love, just as Christ loved us and gave himself for us."

The Ephesians have "kindled" their innate (or "natural") task (to send their representatives to Smyrna) in the blood of God (cf. Acts 20:28); Christ's blood is identified with love (Trall. 8:1; Rom. 7:3), or related to it (Smyrn. 1:1), and have perfectly accomplished it (cf. Smyrn. 11:1).

Ignatius means that their work was that of hastening to see him. This took place when they had heard of his being sent from Syria on behalf of the common name (Christian, cf. 3:1) and hope

2 As for my fellow slave Burrhus, your deacon according to God's will, in every respect blessed, I beg that he may stay on with me for your honor and the bishop's. And Crocus, worthy of God and of you, whom I accepted as an example of your

---

(Jesus Christ, cf. 21:2; Magn. 11:1; Trall. inscr.; 2:2; Philad. 5:2; 11:2; Smyrn. 10:2; 1 Tim. 1:1). He explains that his concern is not only communal but also personal: he hopes (cf. Rom. 1:1) that by their common prayer for him (Eph. 11:2; Magn. 14:1; Philad. 5:1; 8:2; Smyrn. 11:1) he may attain (usually to God, ultimately also here) to fighting wild beasts at Rome (cf. Trall. 10:1; Rom. 4:1–5:3; Smyrn. 4:2) and thus can attain to being a (real) disciple (cf. on 3:1).

He received the whole congregation (Magn. 6:1; Trall. 1:1) in the representative person of the bishop (cf. Smyrn. 8:2) Onesimus. Since Onesimus himself possesses "inexpressible love," Ignatius beseeches them "by Jesus Christ" (cf. Paul, Rom. 15:5 for a similar phrase; 1 Cor. 15:15 for a similar meaning) to love him and to be like him. A doxology follows: "blessed is he" (God) who graciously gave you the favor of being worthy of obtaining such a bishop. On the Old Testament background of such doxologies see E. J. Bickerman, "Bénédiction et Prière," *Revue biblique* 69 (1962), 524-532.

2:1–2. Ignatius wants his "fellow slave" Burrhus to stay with him; this deacon had come to Smyrna from Ephesus, and was later sent to Troas by the Ephesians and Smyrnaeans to act as Ignatius' scribe or to carry some of his letters (Philad. 11:2; Smyrn. 12:1; cf. also Magn. 15:1; Trall. 13:1; Rom. 10:1—mention of Ephesians as present), presumably because he wanted to write to all the churches (Rom. 4:1). Ignatius fairly often refers to deacons, either individually or collectively, as "fellow slaves with me" (Magn. 2:1; Philad. 4:1; Smyrn. 12:2), that is, slaves of Jesus Christ; compare Paul's Colossians 4:7 "Tychicus . . . the beloved disciple and faithful minister [deacon] and fellow slave in the Lord." As usual, Ignatius is identifying himself with Paul, who calls himself a "deacon" in 1 Corinthians 3:5; 2 Corinthians 3:6; 6:4; 11:23; Colossians 1:23, 25; Ephesians 3:7—although without any idea of a particular "office." Burrhus is also described as "blessed," a word repeated, in a different form from the preceding sentence (1:3). His remaining with Ignatius would be "to the honor of yourselves and the bishop"; this is one of two cases in Ignatius' letters where the honor of anyone but God or Christ is mentioned (Eph. 21:1-2; Magn. 3:2; 15:1; Trall. 12:2; Smyrn. 11:2; Polyc. 5:2), although the apostles are mentioned with the Father and Jesus Christ in Trallians. "Honor" is especially characteristic of liturgical expressions (chiefly doxologies); cf. Revelation 4:11; 5:13; 7:12; 1 Clement 61:1-2, 64:1; 65:2. It can be used, however, of persons, as here and, in reference to the same circumstances, in Philadelphians 11:2.

Crocus is also mentioned in Romans 10:1 (the only person with Ignatius to be named in that letter) as a prominent Ephesian. He is

love, has refreshed me in every way; may the Father of Jesus Christ refresh him. With him came Onesimus and Burrhus and Euplus and Fronto, through whom I have seen you all in love. 2. May I always have joy from you [cf. Philem. 20], if only I am

---

"worthy of God" (like the Ephesian presbytery, Eph. 4:1, and the martyrs from Syria, Rom. 10:2); Ignatius is so fond of this expression that he coins the word "Godworthy" and uses it five times (bishop, Magn. 2:1; Smyrn. 12:2; church, Trall. inscr.; faces, Rom. 1:1). "Worthy of God and of you" occurs again in Romans 10:2. Crocus is an exemplar or model of the Ephesians' love; Ignatius elsewhere uses the (Latin) word of Polybius, bishop of Tralles (Trall. 3:2), and of his scribe Burrhus (Smyrn. 12:1). Crocus has refreshed Ignatius "in every way"; Ignatius never uses the verb "to refresh" without the adverbial expression "in every way" or its equivalent (Magn. 15:1; Trall. 12:1; Rom. 10:2; Smyrn. 9:2; 10:1; 12:1), thus suggesting that he is using a formula expressive of gratitude (for Pauline parallels see 1 Cor. 16:18; 2 Cor. 7:13; Philem. 7, 20). *Anapauein* and *anapsychein,* as in Philemon, have the same meaning for Ignatius, both here and in Trall. 12:1-2. He received "refreshment" from the Ephesians, the Smyrnaeans, and the Magnesians; his followers Philo and Rheus Agathopus also received it from the Smyrnaeans (Smyrn. 10:1), and the Syrians at Rome will receive it from the Roman church (Rom. 10:2). On the other hand, neither the Trallians (Trall. 12:1-2) nor the Philadelphians (Philad. 6:3) "refreshed" Ignatius, and the heterodox generally have no care for prisoners (Smyrn. 6:2).

With the expression of gratitude Ignatius combines an expression of hope "that the Father may also refresh him" (for such expressions of reciprocity see on Polyc. 6:1; a close parallel occurs in Smyrn. 9:2).

Onesimus (1:3) and Burrhus (vs. 1) have already been mentioned; Euplus and Fronto appear only here. In their persons Ignatius saw the whole community represented (Eph. 1:3; Magn. 2:1; 6:1). He saw all of them "with love," a word more frequent in Ignatius' letters (43 times) than in all the other Apostolic Fathers (35 times). Usually he speaks of the love of Christians for one another or, less frequently, for God, though once (Rom. 7:3) the blood of Christ is described as "imperishable love," and he says that Christ loves the Church (Polyc. 5:1). In ten instances love is associated with faith. In general, see Richardson pp. 17-22; Corwin pp. 240-244; and J. Colson, "Agape chez Saint-Ignace d'Antioche," *Texte und Untersuchungen* 78 (1961), 341-353.

Several features of Ignatius' style and thought are conspicuously present in this section. First, there is his play on words in relation to Onesimus (Onesimus resembles *onaimēn,* "may I have joy"), apparently borrowed from Paul's letter to Philemon, 20. We may doubt, however, that this coincidence proves that Onesimus of Ephesus is the same person as the runaway slave of Paul's letter; Ignatius repeats the sentence almost exactly in Magnesians 12:1. Second, the question about

worthy. It is fitting, then, in every way to glorify Jesus Christ,
who glorified you, so that you may be made perfect in a single
obedience to the bishop and the presbytery and be sanctified in
every respect.

Ignatius' worthiness recurs in almost every other letter (not Philadelphians), sometimes in relation to a reminiscence of 1 Corinthians
15:9, sometimes not. Third, the expression "it is fitting" is quite common in the letters, usually in regard to obedience to the bishop (Eph.
4:1; Magn. 3:1, 2; Trall. 12:2; Polyc. 5:2) or the appointment of an
emissary (Philad. 10:1; Smyrn. 11:2; Polyc. 7:2), sometimes of assisting
martyrs (Rom. 10:2) or avoiding heretics (Smyrn. 7:2), or of being
genuine Christians (Magn. 4:1). Fourth, the expression of reciprocity
in the sentence about glorifying Jesus Christ is typically Ignatian (see
on Polyc. 6:1). In this instance the act of the Christian is in response
to a prior act of Christ, though this does not seem to be the case in
any other passage where a present action is counseled in view of a
future benefit. (Smyrn. 9:1, "He who honors the bishop has been
honored by God," is past in form but future in sense.) The expression
"having been made perfect" (with reference to unity, 1 Cor. 1:10) recurs in Philadelphians 8:1 (Ignatius is "completely intent upon"
unity) and Smyrnaeans 1:1 (the Smyrnaeans have been "made perfect"
in faith). The Ephesians are to be subject to the bishop (as to God,
Eph. 5:3) and to the presbytery (so Eph. 20:2; Magn. 2:1; 6:1-2; 13:
2; Trall. 2:2; Philad. 7:1; Smyrn. 8:1). In this way they will be "in
every respect consecrated." The verb "to consecrate" occurs only here
and in 12:2 (Paul the "consecrated"), while the cognate adjective
"holy" is relatively rare. It is used once of the Christian "saints"
(Smyrn. 1:2), twice of the "Holy" Spirit (Eph. 18:2; Philad. inscr.),
once of the church (Trall. inscr.), once of the Old Testament Holy of
Holies (Philad. 9:1), once of the Old Testament prophets (Philad.
5:2), and once of the church's presbyters (Magn. 3:1). Holiness is
not a key concept in Ignatius' thought. Similarly, and as in the
Johannine writings, "spirit" is not central (cf. Corwin pp. 141-144).
It is in this section that Ignatius first mentions the "presbytery." The
term also occurs, probably in reference to a group of presbyters or
elders, in 1 Timothy 4:14 (cf. P. Katz in *Zeitschrift für die neutestamentliche Wissenschaft* 51 [1960], 27-30; J. Jeremias, *ibid.* 52 [1961],
101-104). In Ignatius' letters it certainly refers to a group which, together with the bishop (with which it is in harmony, Eph. 4:1), gov-
erns local communities (Eph. 20:2; Magn. 2:1; 13:1; Trall. 2:2; 7:2;
13:2; Philad. 4:1; 7:1; Smyrn. 8:1; 12:2). The presbytery is analogous
to the New Testament apostles (Philad. 5:1); just so, Ignatius compares the "presbyters" to these apostles even when he does not use the
word "presbytery" (Magn. 6:1; Trall. 3:1; cf. 12:2). He does not say
that the presbytery should obey the bishop, but he does say that the
presbyters should do so (Magn. 3:1) or should "refresh" him (Trall.

B. Exhortation to the Ephesians (3:1-2)

3 I am not giving you commands as if I were someone. For even though I am in bonds for the Name, I am not yet perfect in Jesus Christ; for now I am beginning to be a disciple, and I speak to you as my fellow students. For I needed to be anointed by you with faith, instruction, endurance, patience. 2. But since love does not let me be silent about you, I have undertaken to exhort you [cf. Philem. 9], so that together you may run your race in accordance with God's purpose. For Jesus Christ, our inseparable life, is the expressed purpose of the Father, just as the bishops who have been appointed throughout the world exist by the purpose of Jesus Christ.

C. Unity with the Bishop (4:1–6:1)

4 Therefore it is fitting for you to run your race together with

---

12:2; on "refresh" see above). As a group, the presbyters are compared with the "council of God" and the "college of the apostles" (see on Trall. 3:1).

3:1–2. Ignatius does not give orders as if he were someone important (parallels in Trall. 3:3 [an apostle] and Rom. 4:3 [Peter and Paul]); even though he is in bonds for the Name (of Christ, or Christian), he is not yet complete (cf. Philad. 5:1; he can, however, know heavenly matters [Trall. 5:2], and by God's mercy he is someone [Rom. 9:2]). He is only beginning to be a disciple (so 1:2; Rom. 4:2; 5:3) and he addresses his readers as his fellow students (cf. John 11:16 for a similar word; Barn. 1:8 for a similar thought; other references in Bauer p. 203). He needed to be anointed by them with four Christian virtues, the last two of which are especially significant for a martyr (cf. Smyrn. 12:2).

His love for them compels him to speak of them and (therefore) he exhorts them (Trall. 6:1; 12:2; Rom. 4:1; 7:2; Philad. 8:2; Polyc. 1:2; a similar word in Magn. 6:1; Smyrn. 4:1) to "run" (the race of true life, cf. 4:1; Magn. 7:2; Polyc. 6:1) together with, hence in accordance with, the purpose or will of God (Philad. 1:2; Smyrn. 6:2; Polyc. 1:1; 8:1; of Jesus Christ, Philad. inscr.; of the bishop, Eph. 4:1; Polyc. 4:1; 5:2; opposing, Philad. 3:3; 6:2). This involves unity, for Jesus Christ, our "inseparable life" (cf. Magn. 15:2; Trall. 1:1; also Rom. inscr., Philad. inscr.), is the Father's purpose or will and, in turn, the bishops, appointed everywhere (cf. Philad. inscr.), express the will of Jesus Christ. In Ignatius' view, therefore, episcopacy is actually universal and derives its origin from Jesus.

4:1–2. Chapter 4 is one long musical metaphor, though it begins

the bishop's purpose—as you do. For your presbytery—worthy of fame, worthy of God—is attuned to the bishop like strings to a lyre. Therefore by your unity and harmonious love Jesus Christ is sung. 2. Each of you must be part of this chorus so that, being harmonious in unity, receiving God's pitch in unison, you may sing with one voice through Jesus Christ to the Father, so that he may both hear you and recognize you, through what you do well, as members of his Son [cf. 1 Cor. 12:27]. Therefore it is profitable for you to be in blameless unison, so that you may always participate in God [cf. 1 Cor. 10:17].

5 For if in a short time I had such fellowship with your bishop as was not human but spiritual, how much more blessed do I consider you who are mingled with him as the Church is with Jesus Christ and as Jesus Christ is with the Father, so that all things are harmonious in unison! 2. Let no one deceive himself [1 Cor. 6:9]: unless a man is within the sanctuary, he lacks the bread of God [John 6:33; cf. 1 Cor. 9:13; 10:18]. If the prayer of one or two has such power [Matt. 18:19-20], how much more does that of the bishop and the whole church? 3. Therefore he who does not come to the assembly is already proud and has separated himself [cf. 1 Cor. 11:20, 31]. For it is written, "God opposes the proud" [Prov. 3:34; cf. 1 Pet. 5:5; Jas. 4:6]. Let us, therefore, be eager not to oppose the bishop, so that we may be subject to God.

---

with the idea of "running together" with the bishop—a notion based on foot races (cf. 3:2; Magn. 7:2; Polyc. 6:1; for the idea that the Ephesians are already doing what Ignatius requests, see on 8:1). They are living in harmony because the presbytery is "attuned to the bishop like strings to a lyre." The figure recurs in Philadelphians 1:2 (cf. also Rom. 2:2). Under these circumstances "Jesus Christ is sung"; compare Pliny's mention of *carmen Christo quasi deo* (*Ep.* 10, 96, 7; Christian examples in Bauer p. 204; Eph. 5:19; 1 Tim. 3:16; Rev. 5:9, 12; 15:3; 19:6-8). The hymn, however, is in "the key of God" and is addressed to the Father; its consequence is God's recognition of the Ephesians as "members of his Son" (cf. Rom. 12:4; 1 Cor. 6:15; 12:12-27; Eph. 5:30; 1 Clem. 37:5–38:1; 46:7). Christ is the head of these members (Trall. 11:2). The Ephesians must remain in "blameless" (seven times in Ignatius, seven times in 1 Clement) unity so that they may "participate in God" (cf. 1 Cor. 10:17, 21: Eucharistic unity).

5:1–3.   Explicit a fortiori arguments occur rather rarely in Ignatius' letters (cf. 6:1; 16:2). Here (vs. 1-2) we encounter two of them. Igna-

6 And the more anyone sees the bishop being silent, the more one should fear him. For everyone whom the master of a house sends for his stewardship, we must receive as the one who sent him [John 13:20; Matt. 10:40]. It is obvious, then, that one must look upon the bishop as the Lord himself [cf. Gal. 4:14].

---

tius' fellowship (*synētheia*, only here; cf. 1:3) with the bishop was of short duration; that of the Ephesians with him is more durable and more intense; it resembles the union of the Church with Christ (4:2; cf. Polyc. 5:1) and that of Christ with the Father (Magn. 1:2; 6:1; 7:1-2; Rom. 3:3; Smyrn. 3:3). "Harmonious" and "unison" are repeated from 4:1-2.

The argument in verse 2 seems to be based on Pauline phrases. (1) Only those within the sanctuary eat what belongs to the sanctuary (cf. 1 Cor. 9:13)—that is, what is sacrificed there (1 Cor. 10:18); (2) the Christian sacrifice is the bread of God, that is, the flesh of Jesus (John 6:33, 51; cf. Smyrn. 7:1; 1 Cor. 10:16-17); (3) it is offered by the prayer of the bishop in the name of the congregation (Smyrn. 8:1); (4) the prayer is powerful because it more than fulfills the requirement of "one or two" ("two or three" in Matt. 18:20); and Jesus is therefore "in their midst" (Matt. 18:20) as the bread of God.

He who does not join in the Eucharistic assembly (cf. Smyrn. 7:1) has "judged himself" (a curious echo of 1 Cor. 11:31, where the sense is different). Therefore we must not oppose the bishop, who stands in God's place (Magn. 2:1; 6:1; Trall. 3:1); to be subject to him is to be subject to God. Similarly, the sentence from Proverbs is quoted in 1 Peter 5:5 in regard to obedience to "presbyters" by younger men.

In Ignatius' arguments two lines of argument are evidently combined: (1) schismatics lack efficacious sacraments (cf. Smyrn. 8:1-2), and (2) schismatics are hostile toward God (cf. Trall. 7:1-2).

6:1. Why was the bishop of Ephesus "silent"? Lightfoot p. 46 speaks of "the quiet and retiring disposition of the bishop," while Bauer p. 206 suggests that he did not have "the gift of eloquence." H. Chadwick, on the other hand (*Harvard Theological Review* 43 [1950], 167–172), considers all the passages in which Ignatius speaks of silence and concludes that here he is alluding to the bishop's likeness to God, of whom one characteristic is silence (Valentinians, Irenaeus, *Adv. haer.* 1, 11, 1; 2, 12, 2; Clement, *Exc. ex Theod.* 29; magical papyri, cf. Schlier pp. 37-38; other passages in Ignatius, Magn. 8:2; Eph. 19:1). P. Meinhold (*Festgabe J. Lortz II* [Baden-Baden, 1958], 467-490) argues that the Ephesians, like the Philadelphians (1:1) are concerned about a bishop who lacks spiritual gifts, cannot pray or prophesy spiritually, and is forced to remain silent. In Meinhold's view Ignatius defends the bishop by interpreting his silence in semi-Gnostic fashion.

Ignatius' argument is really rather *ad hoc*, since he himself possesses spiritual knowledge (Trall. 5:2) and can speak with God's voice, that is, the Spirit can speak through him (Philad. 7:1-2).

D. The orthodoxy of the Ephesians (6:2–10:3)

2. Indeed, Onesimus himself highly praises your orderliness in God, because you all live in accordance with the truth and because no heresy dwells among you; indeed, you do not even listen to anyone unless he speaks truly of Jesus Christ.

7 For there are some who with wicked guile are accustomed to bear the Name but behave in ways unworthy of God. You must avoid them as wild beasts, for they are mad dogs, biting in secret; you must be on guard against them, for they are practically incurable. 2. There is one Physician:

both flesh and spirit,
begotten and unbegotten,
in man, God,
in death, true life,
both from Mary and from God,
first passible and then impassible,
Jesus Christ our Lord.

No "Gnostic" argument is given here, however, except perhaps by implication. The one whom God ("the master") sends is to be received as God himself (cf. John 13:20 [20:21]; Matt. 10:40). So the bishop is to be regarded as "the Lord himself"—probably, in view of Ignatius' usage elsewhere, and the two Gospel sayings just mentioned, Christ; but Christ is God. Ignatius admits that the situation in Ephesus is not one in which heresy is rampant. Onesimus himself has informed him that the Ephesian Christians live "in accordance with the truth" (the truth of revelation as in John 8:32-33; 16:13, etc.) and (therefore) there is no heresy (Trall. 6:1) among them. The translation of the last sentence is based on the text as emended in the light of the Armenian version by Lightfoot and Hilgenfeld.

7:1–2.   There actually are heretical Christians who wander about (Bauer p. 206 notes Eph. 11:2; Magn. 1:2; Trall. 12:2) and "bear the Name" (cf. 3:1) of Christ or "Christian" (cf. Magn. 4:1), though some of their actions are unworthy of God—in contrast to the actions of Jesus (Eph. 15:1), which, like those of true Christians (Smyrn. 11:3), and true Christians themselves (Eph. 2:1; 4:1; Rom. 10:2), are worthy of God. For Ignatius' own "worthiness" see on 2:2. Such men are wild beasts (in human form, Smyrn. 4:1), like the beasts which Ignatius expects to fight at Rome. More specifically, they are mad dogs (cf. the "leopards" of Rom. 5:1 and the "wolves" of Philad. 2:2) whose bite is hard to cure. Mention of such sickness (cf. 20:2, the Eucharist as

8 So let no one deceive you [2 Thess. 2:3]—as indeed you are not deceived, since you belong entirely to God. For when there is

---

medicine; Trall. 6:2; 11:1, heresy as poison; Polyc. 2:1, cures) leads Ignatius to mention the one Physician, in union with whom the many believers can be cured (cf. Bauer p. 207).

This Physician is described in a series of paradoxes which point toward his "nature" or "origin" as both human and divine. He is at once carnal and spiritual (cf. Smyrn. 3:3; 12:2; so is Polycarp, Polyc. 2:2), born (Eph. 18:2; Magn. 11:1; Trall. 9:1) and not born (only here; a divine attribute), God in man (so patristic quotations; Greek and Latin MSS read "God become incarnate," but Ignatius' style favors the patristic reading), both of Mary and of God (cf. Smyrn. 1:1), first passible and then impassible in the sense that after crucifixion came resurrection (contrast Polyc. 3:2)—Jesus Christ our Lord. The expression "of" or "from" Mary (*ek Marias*) is important; in Galatians 4:4 and Romans 1:3 Paul uses this preposition and Matthew 1:18, 20 speaks of Jesus as "of" the Holy Spirit. Ignatius' usage is the same (Eph. 18:2; Trall. 9:1; Rom. 7:3; Smyrn. 1:1). Valentinian Gnostics spoke of Jesus' origin as "through" Mary and so, occasionally, did Justin Martyr. On the semicredal nature of this passage see Introduction.

8:1–2. Ignatius borrows the Pauline expression (2 Thess. 2:3) "let no one deceive you" and immediately adds "as indeed you are not deceived." This form of expression seems to come from 1 Thessalonians 4:1 (cf. 2 Thess. 3:4), where Paul encourages his readers to continue in their good actions and attitudes. Ignatius frequently employs similar or equivalent expressions, partly (as here) in relation to Pauline injunctions (Rom. 2:1, based on 1 Thess. 2:4; Polyc. 1:2, based on Eph. 4:2), partly in relation to his own (Eph. 4:1; Trall. 2:2; Polyc. 4:1). It may be significant that such phrases are lacking in his letter to the Philadelphians (but cf. Philad. 3:1).

As elsewhere in this letter (18:1) Ignatius uses the Pauline (1 Cor. 4:13) word *peripsēma*. Lightfoot p. 50 points out that it conveys two ideas: (1) "I am the meanest among you," and (2) "I devote my life for you." The connotations are thus both conventional (cf. Barn. 4:9) and sacrificial. But in Ignatius' mind the sacrificial aspect is much the more important. He is sacrificing himself on behalf of the Ephesian church, and thus rather literally identifies himself with the mission of Jesus as described in John 17:18-19. "As thou hast sent me into the world, so I have sent them into the world; and on their behalf I consecrate myself, so that they too may be consecrated in the truth."

Ignatius, as a bishop sent by Christ (Eph. 6:1), must like Christ consecrate himself—for the sake of the church (cf. Paul, Col. 1:24). His spirit is devoted to or for the cross (Eph. 18:1) and for the Smyrnaeans (10:2); that is, he himself is a sacrificial ransom (Eph. 21:1; Polyc. 6:1), a libation poured out to God (see on Rom. 2:2), and, becoming "bread of Christ," a sacrifice (Rom. 4:1-2). It is probably significant

no firmly rooted strife among you that can torment you, you do live in relation to God. I am a sacrifice for you [cf. 1 Cor. 4:13], consecrated for you Ephesians—a church which is famous forever. 2. Men of flesh cannot act spiritually, nor can spiritual men act in a fleshly way, just as faith cannot perform the deeds of unfaith or unfaith those of faith [cf. Rom. 8:5, 8]. But what you do in relation to the flesh is spiritual, for you do everything in Jesus Christ.

9 I have learned to know certain people who had passed by on their way from there with bad teaching: you did not permit them to sow it among you but stopped your ears [Ps. 57:5 LXX] so that you might not receive what they sow. This was because you are stones of the Father's temple [1 Pet. 2:5; cf. 1 Cor. 3:9], made ready for the edifice of God the Father, raised to the heights by the crane—the cross—of Jesus Christ, and using the Holy Spirit for a rope. Your faith is your upward guide and love is the way that leads up toward God. 2. So you are all companions on the way, God-bearers and shrine-bearers, Christ-bearers, bearers

---

that this kind of language occurs only in the letters to those whom he knew best (Ephesians, Smyrnaeans, Polycarp) and to those whom he did not know at all (Romans). Presumably his sacrifice was for the whole Church, but he did not mention it in writing to those who might misinterpret it.

The contrast between carnal and spiritual in verse 2 seems to be based on Pauline language, for example, in Romans 8:5-8 or Galatians 5:17 ff. and the correlation of spirituality with faith is also Pauline (Gal. 5:22). For men without faith or unbelievers compare Magnesians 5:2; Trallians 10:1; Smyrnaeans 2:1; 5:3 (all apparently referring to heretics); in the Magnesians passage they are correlated with "this world." What the Ephesians (essentially spiritual) do in the flesh is spiritual because they do everything in Jesus Christ—just as he, while eating and drinking with his disciples, was spiritually united with the Father (Smyrn. 3:3).

9:1–2. The heretical teachers had evidently come to Smyrna from Ephesus (Bauer p. 208), where they had tried to "sow" (like the tares of Matt. 13:39) their false doctrine; the Ephesians had refused to listen (cf. Trall. 9:1), since they were part of a temple being built for God (cf. Hermas, Vis. 3; Mand. 9—though Hermas is concerned with the quality of the stones, not with the mechanics of construction). See also J. Daniélou, *Primitive Christian Symbols* (Baltimore, 1964), 60-61. Love leads up to the "height" of God according to 1 Clem. 49:4.

of holy things, in every respect adorned with the commandments of Jesus Christ. I rejoice with you, since I have been judged worthy to speak wth you and rejoice with you through what I am writing, for you love nothing in human life, only God.

10 And you must pray unceasingly [1 Thess. 5:17] for the others —for in them is hope for repentance—that they may attain to God. Therefore let them be instructed by you, at least by your deeds. 2. With their wrath you be mild, with their boastful speech you be humble-minded, with their abuse you offer prayers, with their deceit you be firm in faith [cf. Col. 1:23], with their cruelty you be gentle, not eager to imitate them. 3. Let us be found their brothers in our forbearance; let us be eager to be imitators of the Lord [cf. 1 Thess. 1:6], to see who can be the most wronged, defrauded [cf. 1 Cor. 6:7], rejected [Isa. 53:3]—so that no plant of the devil may be found among you but that in complete purity and self-control you may remain in Jesus Christ, in flesh and in spirit.

From the picture of a temple Ignatius' mind turns to that of a religious procession with its "bearers" of various sacred objects, as, for example, in the *kernophoria* at Eleusis (cf. the silver shrines of Artemis at Ephesus [Acts 19:24]). The term *hieraphoros,* "bearing sacred vessels," in the cult of Isis is interpreted metaphorically by Plutarch (*De Iside* 3, p. 352b); so the Christians in their sacred procession (cf. 2 Cor. 2:14) are "adorned" with the commandments of Jesus Christ (cf. Rom. inscr.). Only here and in 15:3 does Ignatius speak of loving God (a similar reticence in Paul [only Rom. 8:28; 1 Cor. 2:9; 8:3]; cf. 1 John 4:7–5:3). The Greek and Latin versions of Ignatius require the translation "in another life"; we have preferred to accept the emendation of Lightfoot.

10:1–3. The "others" whom Ignatius mentions are non-Christians, in whom (as in the "double-minded" of Hermas, Sim. 8, 7, 2) there is still "hope for repentance." Hermas says that if they repent they will live in the tower of the Church; Ignatius says that they may even "attain to God" (see on 12:2). Prayer for non-Christians was frequent in the early Church (see Bauer pp. 209-210).

Ignatius also insists upon Christian behavior: gentleness (cf. Trall. 3:2; 4:2, Polyc. 2:1; 6:2), humble-mindedness (here only in Ignatius; common in 1 Clement), prayer, firmness in faith (Col. 1:23), and mildness (here only in Ignatius). For the general idea compare Matthew 11:29 (of Christ); Matthew 5:44 (of Christians).

The Lord is to be imitated (cf. 1 Thess. 1:6) in his gentleness by suffering wrong in ways mentioned by Paul (1 Cor. 6:7; in turn based

E. Eschatological exhortations (11:1–13:2)

11 These are the last times. Let us then be ashamed and fear God's patience so that it may not become condemnation for us. We should either fear the wrath to come or love the grace which is present, one of the two, just so that we may be found in Christ Jesus for true life. 2. Nothing should seem fitting to you apart from him, in whom I bear my bonds as spiritual pearls. May I rise again in them by your prayer, in which I may always participate so that I may be found in the lot apportioned to the Ephesian Christians, who have always agreed with the apostles by the power of Jesus Christ.

12 I know who I am and to whom I am writing. I am a convict,

---

on something like Matt. 5:39-42) and by being "rejected" (Isa. 53:3). No "plant of the devil" (cf. Matt. 13:38-39; Philad. 3:1; Trall. 11:1) is to be among them; they are to stay in "all purity" (1 Tim. 5:2) and self-control (cf. 1 Clem. 64; Bauer p. 211)—and in Jesus Christ.

11:1–2.   Since Ignatius and his fellow Christians live in "the last times" (cf. 1 Cor. 7:29; 1 John 2:18), they must experience shame and fear of God's patience in postponing judgment. They must either fear the wrath to come (cf. Matt. 3:7; Luke 3:7) or love God's present action of grace. Torrance pp. 77-78 points out that here "Ignatius thinks of grace as the forbearing will of God which has suspended His wrath in the present age, and provided an opportunity for repentance in which we may avail ourselves of His kindness." The idea is thus not unlike that expressed in Paul's Areopagus address (Acts 17:30) or in 1 Thessalonians 1:10: Jesus delivers us from the wrath to come. The fact that Ignatius does not pray for grace to come and for this world to pass away (Did. 10:6, cited by Torrance) simply reflects his "New Testament" emphasis on grace as present: Paul's "by grace you have been saved" (Eph. 2:5).

His rhetorical comparison of chains with pearls may perhaps be based on the parable of the pearl in Matthew 13:45-46; it seems to be imitated by Polycarp (Phil. 1:1). Ignatius will rise not only in the flesh (cf. Trall. 9–10; Smyrn. 2–3) but even in his bonds or fetters and will be found in the "lot" (Philad. 5:1) of the Ephesian Christians (for Christians see on Magn. 10:1), who always agreed with the apostles—especially with Paul (see below).

12:1–2.   Who Ignatius and his readers are is made clear in the sentences that follow, which in form resemble Paul's antithetical statements in 1 Corinthians 4:10 (cf. 2 Cor. 6:10). Ignatius is a "convict" (elsewhere contrasted with being an apostle, Trall. 3:3; Rom. 4:3), while the Ephesians have obtained pardon (from God, cf. 1 Pet. 2:10;

you have been pardoned; I risk danger, you are secure. 2. You are the way for those who are being slain for God—fellow initiates with Paul, the sanctified, the approved, worthy of blessing (may I be found in his footsteps when I reach God!), who in a whole letter makes mention of you in Christ Jesus [Eph. 1:1].

---

1 Tim. 1:13, 16). Ignatius is in danger (of not being a martyr, cf. Trall. 13:3; Paul too was often in danger, 2 Cor. 11:26, though danger could not separate him from the love of God, Rom. 8:35), whereas the Ephesians are secure (since they have always agreed with the apostles, 11:2). Ignatius' language is literal and symbolic at the same time.

They provide a "way" (and therefore are called a way; in 9:1-2 they were on a way) for those "who come to God by a violent death" (A.-G. 54); Ignatius may or may not be generalizing from his own experience with them. They are "fellow initiates" with Paul in the sense that they share in the "mysteries" of Christ's death and resurrection (Magn. 9:2); Paul could call himself "initiated" in speaking of what he had learned from life as an apostle (Phil. 4:12). The language, like that in Ephesians 9:2, is figurative. Ignatius' description of Paul is intended to remind the Ephesians of their vocation. He was sanctified (as all Christians were sanctified, 1 Cor. 6:11) and approved (1 Clem. 47:4), and worthy of blessing (like the Ephesians, inscr.; and Romans, inscr. and 10:1, Christians). Ignatius hopes that he may walk in Paul's footsteps (a figurative expression, as in Sir. 21:6 and Philo, *Opif.* 144, favored by Paul himself, Rom. 4:12; 2 Cor. 12:18; of following Jesus, 1 Pet. 2:21; of following Polycarp, Mart. Polyc. 22:1). Paul mentioned the Ephesians either in every letter (an exaggeration) or in a whole letter (presumably Ephesians); for "in Christ Jesus" see the Pauline Ephesians 1:1 and Introduction.

Ignatius, like Paul, is going to "reach God." Ignatius' use of *tynchanein* ("attain" or "reach") is chiefly in relation to God (Eph. 10:1; Magn. 1:2; Smyrn. 9:2) but also in regard to a harbor or haven (Smyrn. 11:3) and to "a better freedom" (Polyc. 4:3; cf. "a better resurrection," Heb. 11:35). He employs the simple form when he speaks of others, the compound form—perhaps emphatic—when he refers to himself (19 instances)or, once, to Polycarp (2:3). All the passages in which the compound form (*epitynchanein*) occurs either speak directly of attaining to God or Jesus Christ or else refer to the means by which this goal will be achieved.

This usage lies close to that reflected in Luke 20:35 ("those who have been judged worthy of attaining to that age and the resurrection from the dead"), 2 Timothy 2:10 ("I endure everything for the elect so that they may attain to the salvation which is in Christ Jesus with eternal glory"), and Hebrews (6:15, "the promise"; 11:33, "promises"; 11:35, "resurrection"). To "attain" means primarily to participate in God's new age. A different verb (*katantein*) with the same meaning

13 Therefore be eager to meet more frequently for thanksgiving
and glory to God. For when you frequently come together, the
powers of Satan are destroyed and his destructive force is annihilated by the concord of your faith. 2. Nothing is better than
peace, by which all warfare among heavenly and earthly beings
is abolished.

F. The consequences of faith and love (14:1–16:2)

14 None of this escapes your notice if you have perfect faith
and love toward Jesus Christ; these are the beginning and end

---

occurs in Philippians 3:10-11: "taking on the form that he took through
his death, if somehow I may attain to the resurrection from the dead."
Ignatius' language is thus based on previous Christian usage; what he
means is expressed in the words of the "living water" (Rom. 7:2):
"Come to the Father." No one comes to the Father except through
Jesus (John 14:6), whose "way" is the way of sacrificial love (cf.
Eph. 9:1).

13:1–2. Ignatius, like other early Christian writers, recommends
more frequent assemblies (cf. Polyc 4:2; Did. 16:2; 2 Clem. 17:3;
Clem. hom. 3, 69). These assemblies take place "for thanksgiving to
God and for (his) glory." The word for "thanksgiving" is *eucharistia*,
and Ignatius may have the Eucharist in mind; heretics abstain from it
(Smyrn. 7:1). Christian actions generally (Polyc. 5:2), but group
activities especially, take place to God's glory (Magn. 15:1; Rom. 10:2;
Polyc. 7:2) or his honor (Eph. 21:1; Trall. 12:2; Smyrn. 11:2).

When frequent assemblies occur, the powers (angels?) of Satan
(named only here; Satan is so styled by Jesus, as Justin, *Dialogue*
103, 5, points out) are destroyed; his destructive force (only here, but
see 1 Cor. 10:10) is annihilated by the concord of faith (concord mentioned in the triad "faith, love, concord," Philad. 11:2; elsewhere usually "God's concord"). By peace all warfare among heavenly and
earthly beings is abolished. Ignatius likes the expression "there is nothing better than . . ." (Magn. 7:1, Jesus Christ; Polyc. 1:2, "unity")
or its equivalent, "nothing is preferable to . . ." (Magn. 1:2, union of
faith and love; Smyrn. 6:1, faith and love), but he rarely uses the noun
"peace" (in a benediction, Smyrn. 12:2) or the cognate verb (once of
the Trallians, three times of the church at Antioch). Probably "peace"
is too abstract; he prefers "unity," "harmony," or "love."

To judge from this passage and Trallians 4:2, the warfare of which
Ignatius speaks is primarily that waged by the devil against Christians;
he desires to lead them into captivity (see on 17:1).

14:1–2. None of these matters (related to the harmony, faith, and
peace discussed in ch. 13) is hidden (cf. 15:3, "nothing is hidden from

of life, for the beginning is faith and the end is love. When the two exist in unity it is God, and everything else related to goodness is the result. 2. No one who professes faith sins, nor after obtaining love does he hate. The tree is manifest from its fruits [Matt. 12:33]. So those who profess to belong to Christ [cf. 1 Cor. 1:12] will be recognized by what they do. For a deed is not a matter of professing now but of continuing to the end by the power of faith.

15 It is better to be silent and exist than to speak and not exist. It is good to teach if one does what one says. So there is one teacher who "spoke and it happened" [Ps. 32:9 LXX], and

---

the Lord," and 19:1, three mysteries hidden from the prince of this age) if faith and love toward Jesus Christ are perfect (perfect faith, Smyrn. 10:2; perfect love, 1 John 4:18). Faith is the beginning of (true, Christian) life, while love is its end: this is a common Christian doctrine (Bauer p. 213). When faith is united with love, God is present; compare 1 John 4:8: "He who does not love does not know God; for God is love" (see A. Nygren, *Agape and Eros* [London, 1953], 261). Everything else leading to "nobility of character" (*kalokagathia;* in Philo but here only in early Christian literature) is consequent upon faith and love.

Ignatius continues his emphasis upon the consequences of love by combining Johannine and synoptic ideas. No one who professes faith sins, nor does he who has obtained love hate, just as in 1 John (3:6) everyone who remains in him (Christ) does not sin (cf. 1 John 5:18); the contrast between hate and love is especially clear in Matthew 24:10-12. Following Matthew 12:33 or oral tradition (Koester pp. 42-43), Ignatius states that "the tree is known from its fruit." Professed faith must be expressed in love, and he who expresses it by the power given by faith will be saved if he endures to the end (Matt. 10:22; 24:13). To be sure, Ignatius does not mention salvation or endurance, but they seem to be implied both here and in Romans 10:3 (where endurance is mentioned).

The word for "sin" occurs only here and in Smyrnaeans 7:1. There he seems to be using a credal formula (cf. 1 Cor. 15:3); here he is almost certainly dependent upon Johannine thought.

15:1–3. Ignatius now combines two themes: (1) the superiority of deeds to words (14:2; cf. 10:1) and (2) the superiority of silence to words (cf. 6:1). He identifies reality with action, laying emphasis on the effective word of Jesus, understood as the creative speaker in Psalm 32:9 LXX (verse 6 says, "By the word of the Lord the heavens were made"; cf. Theophilus, *Ad Autol.* 1, 7). Jesus' deeds in silence

even what he has done in silence is worthy of the Father. 2. He who has truly acquired the word of Jesus can also hear his silence, so that he may become perfect and act through what he says and be known through what he does not say. 3. Nothing escapes the Father's notice; even our secrets are near him. We should therefore do everything on the assumption that he dwells in us [1 Cor. 3:16], so that we may be his temples and he may be our God in us [cf. 1 Cor. 14:25]—as is the case, and as will be manifest before our face by the effects of the love which we justly bear toward him.

16 Make no mistake, my brothers: those who corrupt families will not "inherit the kingdom of God" [1 Cor. 6:9-10; cf. 3:17]. 2. Then if those who do this in the flesh are to die, how much more so if by wicked teaching someone corrupts faith in God, for which Jesus Christ was crucified? [Cf. Gal. 3:1-3.] Such a man becomes filthy and will go to the unquenchable fire—as will the man who listens to him.

—chiefly his crucifixion (1 Pet. 2:22-23)—are worthy of the Father, for he did nothing apart from him (Magn. 7:1).

The man who really possesses the word of Jesus, the gospel (cf. Tit. 1:3; Col. 3:16; Philad. 11:1), can hear his silence and become perfect (14:1, in faith and love), acting through his own profession of faith and known through his own deeds of love.

God knows men's silent thoughts (cf. 1 Clem. 27:6–28:1), their "secrets" (Magn. 3:2; Philad. 7:1; 9:1). Therefore men must act on the ground that he dwells in them; they are his "temples" (1 Cor. 3:16-17; 6:19; 2 Cor. 6:16); he is their God in them (1 Cor. 14:25). This possibility is an actuality, expressed in the Christians' love for God (Jesus Christ, 14:1). See on 9:2.

16:1–2. Ignatius now turns to warn his readers in the manner of Paul (1 Cor. 3:16-17). As in Philadelphians 3:3, he combines a phrase from 1 Corinthians 15:33 ("make no mistake") with a statement from 1 Corinthians 6:9-10 about those who will not "inherit the kingdom of God," interpreting it in relation to the heterodox and the schismatics. The "families" which are being corrupted are presumably the temples of Jesus, as in 15:3 (Bauer p. 214; also based on 1 Cor. 6:19). Ignatius' thought moves on two levels, the literal (corruption = fornication) and the spiritual (corruption = heresy).

Those who corrupt on the literal level have died (1 Cor. 10: 5-10; for "died" cf. John. 6:49); a fortiori (as in Eph. 5:1-2) those who corrupt faith in God (cf. 14:1; of 25 examples of "faith"

G. God's plan in the work and life of Jesus (17:1–20:2)

17 The Lord received ointment on his head for this reason—
that he might breathe imperishability upon the Church [cf. John
12:3; 20:22]. Do not be anointed with the evil odor of the prince

---

in the letters, 13 occur in Ephesians)—for which Jesus Christ was
crucified (cf. "faith which exists through him," Philad. 8:2)—will go,
defiled (Rev. 22:11), to "the unquenchable fire" (Matt. 3:12; Mark
9:43; Luke 3:17; 2 Clem. 17:7). Anyone who keeps listening to such
teachers will suffer the same fate. The Ephesians do not do so (6:2).

17:1–2. It is possible that the sequence chrismation/baptism occurs
in Ephesians 17–18 because this was the sequence of Christian rites
in Syria (cf. R. H. Connolly, *Didascalia Apostolorum* [Oxford, 1929],
xlviii-l, 146; T. W. Manson in *Journal of Theological Studies* 48 [1947]
59-61). In any event, Ignatius says that the Lord (this term, eight
times in Ephesians, may suggest the presence of traditional language)
received ointment on his head (Matt. 26:7; Mark 14:3) in order to
"breathe" (John 20:22) imperishability on the Church (cf. Clement,
Exc. ex Theod. 3, 2). He may be thinking of the Johannine version
of the anointing story: "the house was filled with the odor of the ointment" (John 12:3), especially since he goes on to contrast this with
the evil odor of the devil's doctrine. Two points thus become fairly
clear. (1) He is thinking of the ointment not as such but as pre-
signifying the Lord's death, for in his view life comes through this
death (Magn. 9:1; Trall. 2:1; 9:1-2; Rom. 6:1; Smyrn. 1:2; 7:1); in
other words, he is relying on the gospel tradition as found in Matthew,
Mark, and John. (2) Like other allegorizers (e.g. Origen), he is
probably interpreting the "house" of John 12:3 as the Church; such
exegesis thus may go back at least to the end of the first century. The
devil's title, "prince of this age" (19:1; Magn. 1:2; Trall. 4:2; Rom.
7:1; Philad. 6:2; "Satan," Eph. 13:1; "devil," Eph. 10:3; Trall. 8:1;
Rom. 5:3; Smyrn. 9:1), is Pauline in form (Richardson p. 69 compares
1 Cor. 2:6, 8; 2 Cor. 4:4; Eph. 2:2; and Ascension of Isaiah 1:3;
2:4; 10:29, etc.) but Johannine in content; in Ignatius' thought *aiōn*
(age) is essentially the same, in the singular, as *kosmos* (world), as
Romans 6:1 shows (cf. John 12:31; 14:30; 16:11). The devil, like his
agents (Philad. 2:2), is eager to take men captive.

Christians are "prudent" (cf. Polyc. 2:2) because like the Corinthians
(1 Cor. 4:10; 10:15) they have "all" received knowledge (1 Cor.
8:1)—knowledge of God, which is Christ (Col. 2:2). Why then are
they foolishly perishing? (1 Cor. 1:18, cf. the quotations in 1 Corinthians 2.) The gift which the Lord has truly sent is imperishability,
as stated above; just so, Paul speaks of "the gift of God" as "eternal
life" (Rom. 6:23).

Schlier pp. 82-84 adduces a verbal parallel from Irenaeus, *Adv.*

of this age, lest he take you captive from the life set before you.
2. Why are we not all wise [cf. 1 Cor. 4:10], since we have
received the knowledge of God—Jesus Christ? [Col. 2:2.] Why are
we foolishly perishing [1 Cor. 1:18], ignoring the gift which the
Lord has truly sent?

18 My spirit is devoted to the cross, which is a stumbling block
to unbelievers but salvation and eternal life to us [1 Cor. 1:18, 23-

---

haer. 1, 4, 1: according to the Valentinian Gnostics, after Sophia descended she had an "aroma of imperishability left to her by Christ and
the Holy Spirit." Again (1, 6, 1), they said that persons who are
"hylic" (material) cannot receive any "breath of imperishability."
If there is any dependence here, it is that of Valentinians on Ignatius,
for his ideas are based on the gospel tradition and on Paul. For him
as for Christians generally imperishability was not innate; it was a
divine gift.

18:1–2.   Ignatius' spirit is "devoted" (cf. 8:1) to the cross; this
expression for "devoted" is fairly common in Greek but probably
occurred to him because Paul used it in 1 Corinthians 4:13. Certainly
he is thinking in Pauline terms. The cross is a "scandal" (Gal. 5:11)
for unbelievers just as the message of the cross is for those who are
perishing, while "to us who are being saved it is the power of God"
(1 Cor. 1:18)—effecting salvation and eternal life (to be saved and
to have eternal life are the same thing in Mark 10:17-27 and parallels).
Ignatius then quotes 1 Corinthians 1:20 almost exactly, with an allusion to 1 Corinthians 1:19 and to Romans 3:27. Boasting is "excluded"
(Rom. 3:27) because of the plan of God effected in the work of Christ.

"Conceived by Mary in accordance with the plan of God" is
explained in the co-ordinate phrases "of the seed of David" (cf. John
7:42; Rom. 1:3; 2 Tim. 2:8) and "of the Holy Spirit." As Bauer p.
215 points out (cf. *Das Leben Jesu im Zeitalter der neutestamentlichen
Apokryphen* [Tübingen, 1909], 13-15), in the second century Mary
was usually regarded as descended from David—not only in apocryphal literature such as the Protevangelium (10:1, p. 70, 4-5 Testuz)
and 3 Corinthians 5 (the oldest MSS of these documents have been
edited by M. Testuz in *Papyrus Bodmer V: Nativité de Marie* [Geneva,
1958] and *Papyrus Bodmer X-XII Correspondence apocryphe des Co-
rinthiens et de l'apôtre Paul . . .* [Geneva, 1959]), but also by Justin
(*Apology* 1, 32, 14; *Dialogue* 43, 1; 45, 4; 100, 3; 101, 1; 120, 2); Tatian
(*Diatessaron*); Irenaeus (*Adv. haer.* 3, 9, 2; 3, 16, 2; 3, 21, 5; *Demon-
stration* 36), and Clement (*Str.* 1, 147, 5). Presumably the genealogies
in Matthew 1:2-16 and Luke 3:23-38 were regarded as genealogies of
Mary, not of Joseph (whom Ignatius never mentions). See also O.
Cullmann, *The Christology of the New Testament* (Philadelphia, 1959),

24]. "Where is the wise man? Where is the debater? Where is the boasting of the so-called intelligent?" [1 Cor. 1:20.] 2. For our God, Jesus the Christ, was conceived by Mary in accordance with the plan of God—of the seed of David and of the Holy Spirit; he was born and was baptized in order to purify the water by the passion.

19 Both the virginity of Mary and her giving birth escaped the notice of the prince of this age, as did the Lord's death—three

---

127-136, 295-296. On Jesus' origin, according to Ignatius, see also Ephesians 7:2; Trallians 9:1; Romans 7:3; Smyrnaeans 1:1.

Why was he baptized in order to purify the water? In order to understand this passage we must consider the meaning which "pure" and "purify" has for Ignatius. Purity is a characteristic of the divine, of the light of God (Rom. 6:2; of the sanctuary, Trall. 7:2); it is essentially a religious term though it also has a moral connotation ("pure in conscience," Trall. 7:2). It can be attained through suffering (Rom. 4:1; 6:2), which presumably resembles "filtering" in its effects (Rom. inscr.; Philad. 3:1). Water as such is merely material and therefore not pure (cf. Rom. 6:2, contrast between matter and pure light); therefore it was necessary for the Lord to purify the water of baptism by his suffering. And Ignatius could have been aware that baptism was related to suffering if he considered the saying in Mark 10:38-39, in which both "cup" and "baptism" are used in reference to the self-sacrifice, first of Christ and second of his disciples. Just as the Christian dies with Christ in baptism (Rom. 6:3-11; Col. 3:3), so Christ's sufferings were prefigured in his own baptism.

Bartsch p. 139, following Dibelius, emends the text, in our view wrongly.

Compare the Gnostic Gospel of Philip (p. 125, 7-9): "Even as Jesus perfected the water of baptism, so did he pour out death. Because of this we go down indeed into the water, but we do not go down into death, in order that we may not be poured out into the spirit of the world." (For this work cf. R. McL. Wilson, *The Gospel of Philip* [New York, 1962].)

19:1–3. The interpretation of this passage depends, in large measure, on the context in which it is set. Schlier pp. 5-32 and Bartsch pp. 133–159 discuss it primarily in the light of parallels derived from later Gnostic sources; they regard it as the principal "mythological" section in Ignatius' letters. Nock (*Journal of Theological Studies* 31 [1929–30], 310) argued that Ignatius was not a Gnostic and that the existence of a "Gnostic myth" behind this chapter has not been proved; he spoke of "synoptic belief in the atmosphere of Gnosis" and of the "frankly imaginative character of Eph. 19." Corwin pp. 175–188 also rejects the "Gnostic" interpretation, for the passage does not describe

mysteries of a cry, wrought in the stillness of God. 2. How then
was he made manifest to the ages? A star shone forth in heaven
brighter than all the stars, and its light was ineffable and its
novelty produced astonishment; all the other stars, with sun and
moon, gathered in chorus about this star, and it outshone them
all. There was perplexity as to the origin of this novelty, so

---

the descent of the redeemer. In so far as there is mythological material, it is "much closer to Jewish thought than to Mandaean or pre-
Valentinian gnosis" (p. 183).

Chapter 19 consists of two parts. The first deals with "three
mysteries of a cry, wrought in the stillness of God": these were
(1) Mary's virginity, (2) her giving birth, and (3) the Lord's
death; and all of them escaped the notice of "the prince of this
age." What this statement means is that the "prince of this age"
and his allies did not recognize "the Lord of glory" (1 Cor. 2:8);
Ignatius is amplifying a Pauline statement by relating it specifically to Jesus' birth and death. The first cry is probably Mary's
question to the angel Gabriel (Luke 1:34) or perhaps the Magnif-
icat (Luke 1:46-55); the second cry is that of her labor (cf.
John 16:21); the third is Jesus' loud cry at his death (Mark 15:34
or 37). To treat this kind of writing as Gnostic is to assume that
orthodoxy must be unimaginative.

But how were these mysteries worked in God's stillness? Schlier
p. 27 speaks of the stillness as "the sphere of God" (cf. Irenaeus,
Adv. haer. 1, 1, 1; 1, 2, 1). This is right; but the "sphere" is not
necessarily Gnostic. Cabaniss (Vigiliae Christianae 10 [1956], 97-
102) has pointed out an excellent parallel in the Wisdom of
Solomon (18:14-15): "When still silence enclosed everything, and
night in its swift course was now half gone, thy all-powerful word
leaped from heaven, from the royal throne, into the midst of
the land that was doomed. . . ." (See also Magn. 8:2.) This is to
say that Ignatius' language may well be derived from Hellenistic
Judaism (or Christianity) rather than from Gnosticism.

The second part of the chapter deals with the manifestation
of the Lord to "the ages" (Schlier p. 28 insists that Ignatius must
mean Gnostic aeons, but this is uncertain). Reitzenstein, followed
by Schlier p. 31, argued that to the original myth (19:2a) Ignatius
added his own phantasies (19:2b).

19:2a	19:2b
A star *shone* forth in heaven *brighter* than *all the stars,* and its *light* was ineffable and its *novelty* produced astonishment;	*all the* other *stars,* with sun and moon, gathered in chorus about this star, and it *outshone* them *all.* There was perplexity as to the origin of this *novelty,* so unlike the others.

unlike the others. 3. Thus all magic was dissolved and every bond of wickedness [Isa. 58:6] vanished; ignorance was abolished and the old kingdom was destroyed, since God was becoming manifest in human form for the newness of eternal life [Rom. 6:4]; what had been prepared by God [1 Cor. 2:9] had its beginning. Hence everything was shaken together, for the abolition of death was being planned.

20 If Jesus Christ deems me worthy through your prayer, and if it is God's will, in the second brochure which I am going

---

By using this kind of method one can prove almost anything. The phantasies were in the minds of Reitzenstein and Schlier (see Corwin pp. 177–179).

One does better to turn back to the Wisdom of Solomon (7:29-30): "She [wisdom] is more beautiful than the sun, and excels every constellation of the stars. Compared with the light she is found to be superior, for it is succeeded by the night, but against wisdom evil does not prevail."

Is the star the Lord, as the Valentinian Theodotus states (Clem. *Exc. ex Theod.* 74, 2) and as Schlier p. 28 said Ignatius supposed? It is hard to see how this could be, since God was becoming manifest in *human* form (vs. 3). More probably, the star is the star of Bethlehem in Matthew 2:1-12, described in imaginative fashion. As Lightfoot p. 82 remarks, "The symbol and the thing symbolized might be blended together."

We should mention the attempt of Bartsch pp. 156–158 to differentiate "community tradition" and "the myth." He finds the former in these words: "the virginity of Mary and her giving birth (similarly also the Lord's death), three mysteries from which all magic was dissolved and every bond of wickedness vanished; ignorance was abolished and the old kingdom was destroyed, since God was becoming manifest in human form for the newness of eternal life." The latter is expressed in Ignatius' statements about the cry, the prince of this age, and the activities of the stars. When Ignatius introduces these ideas, he transmutes history and eschatology into mythology (Bartsch pp. 158–159). Bartsch does not seem to recognize the "mythological" aspects of what he calls "community tradition."

On this passage see also W. Telfer in *Theology* 27 (1936), 66-72; A. D. Nock in *Journal of Theological Studies* 31 (1929-30), 310-313 (review of Schlier); J. Daniélou, *Primitive Christian Symbols* (Baltimore, 1964), 112-123; D. Daube in *Journal of Theological Studies* 16 (1965), 128–129.

20:1–2. "Prayer" here, as in 1:2 and elsewhere, means primarily the common prayer of the church, emphasized in Eph. 5:2; Magn. 7:1; 14:1; and Trall. 12:2 (private prayer is not excluded,

to write you I will give you the explanation of what I have begun—the divine plan in relation to the new man Jesus Christ, concerning his faith and his love, his passion and resurrection; 2. especially if the Lord reveals to me that individually you are all joining, by grace from the Name, in one faith and in

---

cf. Polyc. 1:3; 2:2). Ignatius hopes to write a second brochure, or "little book," about the divine plan in relation to the "new man Jesus Christ"; the expression "new man" occurs in Paul's Ephesians (2:15; 4:24) in regard to Christians (cf. also 1 Tim. 2:5, "the man Christ Jesus"). He has begun to discuss this, primarily in chapters 17–19; he would like to continue with his faith and his love, his passion and resurrection. Lightfoot p. 86 (so Bauer p. 218) regards the faith and love as "towards him"; Lake and Goodspeed treat them as characteristics of Christ. Magnesians 1:1 favors the former view; Smyrnaeans 10:2 (Jesus Christ is "perfect faith"), the latter. Christ's love is mentioned by Ignatius (Polyc. 5:1, from Eph. 5:25-29) and in the New Testament (e.g., Rom. 8:35; 2 Cor. 5:14; Eph. 3:19; cf. Gal. 2:20); therefore it seems likely that the second interpretation is correct.

Ignatius will write the brochure "if the Lord reveals" to him (since he is not present at Ephesus; cf. Paul's situation, 1 Cor. 5:3-4) that the Ephesians are united "in grace from his name." The expression seems to reflect their acceptance of the apostolic salutation "grace to you . . . from our Lord Jesus Christ" and benediction "grace . . . be with your spirit" (Gal. 6:18; Phil. 4:23; Philem. 25; cf. 2 Cor. 13:14; Eph. 6:24). Torrance p. 79 suggests that the phrase "in grace" indicates "the result of humble unity in which all members of the community submit to the Bishop in faith and discipline." Nothing in the context supports this view, and the parallels he provides from Magnesians 6–7 contain no mention of grace. The consequence of grace is unity of faith and life, expressed in obedience.

Christians meet in the one faith (Paul, Eph. 4:5), that is, belief (cf. Rom. 1:5; Gal. 1:23; Jude 3; Ign. Eph. 16:2; cf. John 20:31), and in the one Jesus Christ (cf. Magn. 7:2; 1 Clem. 46:6), who was humanly descended from David (Trall. 9:1; Smyrn. 1:1; "seed of David," Eph. 18:2; cf. Paul, Rom. 1:3) as "son of man" but was also Son of God. Ignatius is obviously employing the enigmatic expression used in the Gospels by Jesus, not in the context of late Jewish apocalyptic thought—where "Son of man" often means a divine being—but in a context like that of Psalm 8:4 or Ezekiel, where it means "man" (so also Barn. 12:10).

They also obey their presiding officers, the bishop and the presbytery, "with undistracted mind" (cf. 1 Cor. 7:35). Ignatius has already explained the grounds for this obedience in chapters 3–6.

Jesus Christ, who was of the family of David after the flesh [Rom. 1:3], son of man and Son of God, so that you may obey the bishop and the presbytery with undisturbed mind, breaking one loaf [1 Cor. 10:16-17], which is the medicine of immortality, the antidote which results not in dying but in living forever in Jesus Christ.

H. Final greeting (21:1-2)

21 I am devoted to you and to those whom you sent in God's honor to Smyrna, from which I write to you, thanking the

---

The Church is to "break one bread"—in the Lord's Supper or Eucharist (cf. 1 Cor. 10:16; Acts 2:46; probably Luke 24:35). Ignatius identifies the bread as the "medicine of immortality" and antidote for death. There is no reason to suppose that the term was borrowed from Hellenistic mystery religions (so. R. Reitzenstein, *Die hellenistische Mysterienreligionen,* 3d ed. [Leipzig, 1927], 400); such a supposition rests upon a series of conjectures related to the story that Isis discovered such a drug and gave it to her son Horus (Diodorus Siculus 1, 25, 6). Ignatius is saying no more than what is said in John 6:57: "He who eats me will live because of me." Maurer pp. 93–94 argues against Schlier and Bartsch that the passage does not involve "magic" because of its primary emphasis on unity. This is true, but "magic" is not the same as "sacrament," in spite of Lightfoot p. 87: "this very material conception." Ignatius is not far from either John or Paul (1 Cor. 10:16-17; 11:28-31), and "medicine of immortality" is no more literal than "deadly drug" in Trallians 6:2.

21:1–2. "I am devoted to you," Ignatius writes—as also to the other correspondents he knows best (Smyrn. 10:2; Polyc. 2:3; 6:1). The word *antipsychon* is used of a vicarious sacrifice in 4 Maccabees 6:29; 17:22, a work perhaps used in the Jewish community at Antioch in Ignatius' time and dealing with the most famous martyrs of the Maccabaean period (cf. Daniélou p. 53). He is also devoted to the delegates mentioned in chapters 1–2. He writes from Smyrna, where he has had the good fortune to meet a kindred spirit in the bishop Polycarp (cf. Magn. 15:1). The Ephesians are to "remember" or "make mention of" him in their prayers, just as Jesus Christ intercedes with the Father for them, as High Priest (cf. Philad. 9:1).

They should also pray for the church in Syria, presumably that at Antioch in particular (though Ignatius does not mention it in any letter written from Smyrna). He reminds his readers of his journey to Rome (cf. 1:2) and speaks of himself as the "least" of the faithful

Lord and loving Polycarp and you as well. Remember me, as Jesus Christ remembers you. 2. Pray for the church in Syria, from which I am being led in bonds to Rome as the least [1 Cor. 15:9] of the faithful there, since I was judged worthy to serve God's honor. Farewell in God the Father and in Jesus Christ, our common hope [1 Tim. 1:1].

---

in Syria. One might not suppose that he has 1 Corinthians 15:9 in mind, but the parallels in the other letters show that he does (Magn. 14:1; Trall. 13:1; Rom. 9:2; Smyrn. 11:1). Though Ignatius was the least, God chose him for his own honor—to proclaim the faith by martyrdom (cf. Eph. 3:1; 8:1). The closing words speak of God the Father and Jesus Christ (though both can be called God, the Father is not the Son) and refer to Jesus as "our common hope." This expression is perhaps derived from 1 Timothy 1:1 ("Christ Jesus our hope") combined with Titus 1:4 ("common faith"); cf. Ephesians 1:2; Magnesians 11:1; Philadelphians 11:2; Smyrnaeans 10:2.

Corwin pp. 27-29 has well discussed Ignatius' feeling of unworthiness, and concludes that it was because of a struggle at Antioch which Ignatius had failed to resolve (so also Harrison pp. 79-106). Perhaps the church's recovery was partly due to Ignatius' departure. Did he follow Clement's counsel about voluntary exile? (1 Clem. 54-55.) On the other hand, the Pauline parallel may possibly suggest that Ignatius once persecuted the church himself, though this remains purely hypothetical.

The word Ignatius uses for "least" is *eschatos*, while Paul used *elachistos* in 1 Corinthians 15:9. In 1 Corinthians 4:9, however, Paul's *eschatos* ("the apostles last") carries overtones of "least," as the subsequent verses show. Similarly, in the synoptic saying about the first being "last" (*eschatoi*, Matt. 19:30; 20:16; Mark 9:35; 10:31) a connotation of "least" is also conveyed.

MAGNESIANS

OUTLINE

Salutation
A. Ignatius' gratitude for the visit of Damas and others (1:1–2:1)
B. The Magnesian bishop (3:1–4:1)
C. The ways of life and death (5:1-2, a digression)
D. Exhortation to unity (6:1–7:2, continued from 2:1)
E. The problems of the Judaizers (8:1–10:3)
F. The condition of the Magnesian Christians (11:1–13:2)
G. Summary and final greeting (14:1–15:1)

Magnesians

Salutation

Ignatius, also called Theophorus, to her who is blessed by the grace of God the Father in Christ Jesus our Savior, in whom I salute the church which is at Magnesia on the Maeander and wish her abundant greeting in God the Father and in Jesus Christ.

A. Ignatius' gratitude for the visit of Damas and others (1:1–2:1)

1 When I learned of the orderliness of your love toward God, I gladly decided to speak with you in the faith of Jesus Christ. 2. For being judged worthy of a most godly name, in the bonds which I bear I sing of the churches and I pray that in them there may be a union of the flesh and spirit of Jesus Christ, our life

---

Salutation. Next to the one to Polycarp this is the shortest salutation in Ignatius' letters, and, apart from identifying the particular Magnesia to which he writes (cf. Bauer p. 220), does nothing but repeat part of the salutation to the Ephesians ("blessed . . . by the fullness of God the Father") and refer to the "grace" which will later be contrasted with the "Judaism" affecting the Magnesians (8:1-2). The expression "Christ Jesus our Savior" (Eph. 1:1; cf. Smyrn. 7:1) is fairly common in Paul's epistle to Titus (1:4; 2:13; 3:6; cf. 2 Tim. 1:10). Note that in this letter, as in Philadelphians, Jesus Christ is not called God; in both letters Ignatius probably does not wish to multiply difficulties with Judaizers.

1:1–2. Like the Ephesians (Eph. 6:2), the Magnesians are characterized by good order (cf. 1 Clem. 37:2; 42:2), and therefore Ignatius is glad to write to them (cf. Eph. 9:2) in the faith expressed by (Eph. 20:1) and toward (Eph. 1:1; 14:1) Jesus Christ and derived from him (Magn. 9:1; Philad. 8:2).

He has been judged worthy (by God) of bearing a "most godly" (Smyrn. inscr.; 11:1; Polyc. 7:2) name, presumably Theophoros, "God-bearing," since he goes on to speak of bearing his bonds (cf. Eph. 11:2). He sings the praises of the churches just as he urges the Ephesians (Eph. 4:1-2) and the Romans (Rom. 2:2) to sing to the Father. He prays for all-inclusive unity: the flesh of Jesus Christ with his spirit, faith with love, Jesus with the Father (cf. 13:1-2). Nothing is preferable to the union of faith with love (so. Smyrn. 6:1;

57

forever; of faith and love, to which nothing is preferable; and
—most important—of Jesus and the Father. If in him we endure
the whole evil treatment of the prince of this age, and escape,
we shall attain to God.

2 Since, then, I was judged worthy of seeing you through Damas
your Godworthy bishop and the worthy presbyters Bassus and
Apollonius and my fellow slave the deacon Zotion—whom
may I enjoy because he is subject to the bishop as to God's grace
and to the presbytery as to the law of Jesus Christ. . . .

B. The Magnesian bishop (3:1–4:1)

3 And it is fitting for you not to take advantage of the bishop's
youth but to render him full respect in accordance with the power
of God the Father, just as I know that the holy presbyters have
not presumed upon his youthful external appearance but, as

---

elsewhere "nothing is better" than peace, Eph. 13:2; or Jesus Christ,
Magn. 7:1; or unity, Polyc. 1:2; but the meaning of all these terms
is essentially the same). If we endure ("all things," Smyrn. 9:2) the
attacks of the prince of this age (see on Eph. 17:1) we shall attain
to God (see on Eph. 12:2).

2:1. Ignatius repeats the words "since, then" in 6:1 (5:1 is the
same but is correlated with chs. 3–4) and continues with the thought
interrupted at the end of chapter 2. His sentence here is syntactically
incomplete. The idea that he sees the whole congregation representa-
tively is also expressed in Ephesians 1:3 and Trallians 1:1. On deacons
as "fellow slaves" and the word "enjoy," see on Eph. 2:2. Ignatius
elsewhere compares the bishop with God (6:1; Trall. 3:1, etc.) and
both the bishop and the deacons with "the commandment" (of God;
Trall. 13:2; Smyrn. 8:1). See Introduction. The word "law" occurs
only here and in Smyrnaeans 5:1 (the law of Moses). Presumably
Ignatius is mentioning both grace and law simply to point toward
the totality of the Christian religion (cf. John 1:17; not as in Rom.
6:14). Admittedly, however, the parallel between God's grace and the
bishop is rather extreme (so Torrance p. 80).

3:1–2. The bishop's youth (cf. 1 Tim. 4:12) may create difficulties
at Magnesia, as other bishops' silence makes trouble elsewhere (Eph.
6:1; Philad. 1:1; "gentleness," Trall. 3:2). Actually the bishop is em-
powered by the Father and the presbyters really do yield to him and
to the divine Bishop (overseer) of whom he is a copy (cf. 6:1; Eph.
1:3; Trall. 3:1; Rom. 9:1; Polyc. inscr.). Anyone who disobeys the
bishop "cheats" God and will have his account audited by one who
knows even what is secret (cf. Eph. 15:3; Philad. 7:1; 9:1).

men wise in God, yield to him—not to him but to the Father of Jesus Christ, to the bishop of all. 2. For the honor of him who loved us, it is fitting for us to obey without any hypocrisy; for a man does not deceive only this visible bishop but also cheats the invisible one. The reckoning of this account is not with flesh but with God, who knows men's secrets.

4 It is fitting, then, not just to be called Christians but to be such—just as some use the title "bishop" but do everything apart from him. Such men do not seem to me to act in good conscience, since they do not meet validly in accordance with the commandment.

C. The ways of death and life (5:1-2, a digression)

5 Since, then, actions have a consequence and two goals lie before us, death and life, and each is going to go to his own place; 2. for just as there are two coinages, the one of God, the other of the world, and each has its own stamp impressed on it, unbelievers that of this world, believers (with love) the stamp of God the Father through Jesus Christ; and unless we voluntarily choose to die in relation to his passion [cf. Rom. 6:3], his life is not in us [cf. John 6:53].

4:1. To be a Christian is more important than to be called one (Rom. 3:2; cf. 1 Pet. 4:14-16); consequently one cannot simply speak respectfully of or to the bishop while acting "apart from him" (cf. 7:1; Trall. 2:2; 7:2; Philad. 7:2; Smyrn. 8:1-2; Polyc. 4:1). It is clear that, for Ignatius, to have a good or pure conscience is closely related to the correct relations of the congregation to the bishop (Trall. 7:2) or vice versa (Philad. 6:3). "Valid" church meetings are those with the bishop or under episcopal sanction (Smyrn. 8:1), for Jesus Christ provided the "validity" of the ministry by his Holy Spirit (Philad. inscr.) and the ministry is based on his will or purpose (Eph. 3:2).

5:1–2. This chapter is only tenuously related to what precedes and what follows. Actions have consequences, and there are two ways set before men: the way of life and the way of death (cf. Did. 1:1, etc.). In Acts 1:25 Judas went "to his own place."

In verse 2 Ignatius combines the two ways with the two coinages (God's and the world's) found in the gospel story of the tribute money (Mark 12:13-17 and parallels). Schlier p. 133 relies on the fact that Ignatius' idea recurs in Clement of Alexandria (*Exc. ex Theod.* 86; *Eclogae propheticae* 24) as proof that it is Gnostic in

D. Exhortation to unity (6:1–7:2, continued from 2:1)

6 Since, then, in the persons already mentioned [cf. 2:1] I have beheld the whole congregation in faith and have loved it, I exhort you: be eager to do everything in God's harmony, with the bishop presiding in the place of God and the presbytery in the place

---

origin; but *Exc. ex Theod.* 86 probably comes from Clement himself, not from Theodotus (so F. M. Sagnard, *Clément d'Alexandrie: Extraits de Théodote* [Paris, 1949], 210; cf. R. P. Casey, *The Excerpts from Theodotus by Clement of Alexandria* [London, 1935], 8). If there is any borrowing, it is by Clement from Ignatius or from earlier tradition.

One coinage bears the image of "this world" (i.e., of Caesar), the other that of "the Father through Jesus Christ." This is to say that believers constitute the true humanity to which God's image (Jesus himself) has been restored. They must die into or toward his passion so that they may also share in his resurrection. This idea is Pauline; cf. Paul, Romans 6:3-11; Philippians 3:10-11.

6:1–2. Ignatius now picks up the sentence from which he digressed, because of his concern for the Magnesian situation, at the end of chapter 2, and explains that it was "in faith" that he saw the whole congregation in its representatives—and loved them (he associates faith with love very frequently). Because of this, he exhorts them (also very frequent, but except in Smyrn. 4:1 he uses a different verb with the same meaning)—quite specifically—to do everything "in harmony with God" or "in God's harmony" (similarly, 15:1), under circumstances in which the bishop = God (or even, has God's function), the presbyters = the council (synedrion = Sanhedrin) of the apostles (cf. Trall. 3:1; Philad. 8:1), and the deacons ("very sweet," only here, to Ignatius) being entrusted with service to Jesus Christ (cf. Trall. 2:3). Mention of Jesus Christ leads to a kind of doxological statement about him: he was with the Father before the ages (cf. John 1:2; 17:5, 24) and was made manifest ("appeared") at the end (of the ages, cf. 1 Cor. 10:11).

All the Magnesians must therefore act in God's harmony or conform with God (cf. Polyc 1:3) by respecting (presumably equivalent to, or expressing, "loving") one another (cf. Trall. 3:1-2; Smyrn. 8:1); they are not to regard a neighbor (this confirms the idea that love of neighbor underlies Ignatius' words) in a carnal way, but constantly are to love one another (John 13:34; 1 Thess. 4:9; Rom. 12:9-10). There is to be nothing among them which can split them (on "divisions" cf. Philad. 2:1; 3:1; 7:2; 8:1; Smyrn. 7:2; the verb only here); instead they are to be united with the bishop (cf. 13:2) and with those who preside (presumably also the presbyters) as an "example and lesson" (cf. "example of teaching," Paul, Rom. 6:17) of imperishability —because life in and with God is characterized by such unity.

of the council of the apostles and the deacons, most sweet to me, entrusted with the service of Jesus Christ—who before the ages was with the Father and was made manifest at the end. 2. All of you, then, having received a divine agreement in your convictions, admonish one another, and let no one view his neighbor in a merely human way [cf. 2 Cor. 5:16]; but constantly love one another in Jesus Christ. Let there be nothing in you that can divide you, but be united with the bishop and with those who preside, for an example and lesson of imperishability.

7 As, then, the Lord did nothing apart from the Father, either by himself or through the apostles, since he was united with him, so you must do nothing apart from the bishop and the presbyters. Do not try to make anything appear praiseworthy by yourselves, but let there be in common one prayer, one petition, one mind, one hope in love, in blameless joy—which is Jesus Christ, than whom nothing is better. 2. All of you must run together as to one temple of God, as to one sanctuary, to one Jesus

7:1–2. Ignatius now proceeds to provide theological grounding for his doctrine of union with, as subordination to, the bishop. The Lord was united with the Father (John 10:30; 17:11, 21-22) and did nothing apart from the Father, either "through himself" ("of himself," John 5:19, 30; 8:28-29) or through the apostles (John 17:17; 20:21); therefore Christians are to do nothing apart from the bishop (so Trall. 2:2; Philad. 7:2) and the presbyters. They are not to try to make private (sectarian) exercises of worship appear right (compare, perhaps, "private" exegesis as denounced in 2 Pet. 1:21). Instead—and here Ignatius turns from John to Paul—there is to be, in common, a single prayer and petition (in relation to) a single mind and hope (in love and in blameless joy). Ignatius' language recalls that of Paul: "one Lord, one faith, one baptism," etc. (Eph. 4:4-6.) He identifies unity in all these respects with Jesus Christ, "than whom nothing is better" (for this expression see on Eph. 13:2).

In order to reach this goal, Christians must "run together" (an athletic metaphor originally, Eph. 3:2; 4:1; Polyc. 6:1; cf. 1 Cor. 9:24) as to one temple (cf. Eph. 9:1-2), as to one sanctuary (cf. Eph. 5:2 and commentary), and literally to one Jesus Christ. He came forth (Magn. 8:2) from the one Father (John 8:42; 13:3), is with the one (John 1:18), and departed to the one (John 14:12, 28; 16:10, 17).

In this chapter, therefore, Ignatius has woven together the Pauline and Johannine expressions of the theme of unity.

Christ, who proceeded from the one Father and is with the one and departed to the one.

E. The problem of the Judaizers (8:1–10:3)

8 Do not be deceived by strange doctrines [cf. Tit. 1:14] or by antiquated myths, since they are useless. For if we are still living

---

8:1–2. Ignatius' appeal to avoid strange doctrines and antiquated myths is close to that found in the Pastoral Epistles (1 Tim. 1:4; 4:7; 2 Tim 4:4; especially Tit. 1:14: "Jewish myths and human commandments"). To live in conformity with Judaism, after the incarnation, means acknowledging that grace has not been received. This idea is clearly Pauline: Christians justified by the law have fallen from Grace (Gal. 5:4; also Heb. 13:9). Torrance pp. 80-81 wrongly denies the Pauline inspiration of the passage; the *"gratia infusa"* to which he refers is not present in the passage. The words for "old" or "antiquated" occur in Ignatius only here (also 9:1; 10:2) and in Ephesians 19:3. Evidently he regards Judaism as the primary expression of "antiquity" in contrast to the "newness" (9:1; Eph. 19:2-3) of the gospel. This point is important for the exegesis of Ephesians 19 (see commentary).

Torrance gratuitously states that "evidently in the prophets of the Old Testament we have parallels to the Bishops in the Christian churches," but there is nothing here to suggest this. The reason why Judaism is not related to Christian grace is that the Old Testament prophets, "most divine" (only here in Ignatius), really lived "in accordance with Christ Jesus" (cf. Philad. 5:2; 9:1-2), not in accordance with Judaism, for they were persecuted by Jewish leaders (cf. Matt. 5:12; Luke 11:47-51; Acts 7:51-52). They were inspired by Christ's grace (cf. 1 Pet. 1:10-12; Barn. 5:6) to say that "there is one God who manifested himself through Jesus Christ his Son" (cf. 1 Cor. 8:6; John 1:18, etc.). The Son is "his Word which proceeded from silence." (This is the reading of the Armenian version and of the Monophysite Severus; the text of the Greek MS and the Latin version, "eternal Word not proceeding from silence," reflects anti-Gnostic alteration.) Is this Gnostic? (So Bauer p. 225, Schlier pp. 38-39, *et al.*) It seems more likely that the language is based on Wisdom of Solomon 18:14-15 (see on Eph. 19:1-3), as Windisch pointed out (*Neutestamentliche Studien G. Heinrici* [Leipzig, 1914], 234 n. 1). To say with Bauer p. 226 that for Ignatius "God is Silence" is overprecise. His thought resembles that of John 1:18: "No one has ever seen God; the only-begotten God, who is in the Father's bosom, has revealed him." It is this divine Son incarnate who was "pleasing to him who sent him" (John 8:29).

in conformity with Judaism, we acknowledge that we have not received grace [cf. Gal. 5:2, 4]. 2. For the most divine prophets lived in conformity with Christ Jesus. For this reason they were persecuted, though inspired by his grace to convince the disobedient that there is one God who manifested himself through Jesus Christ his Son, who is his Word which proceeded from silence and in every respect pleased him who sent him [John 8:29].

9 If, then, those who lived in antiquated customs came to newness of hope, no longer keeping the Sabbath [cf. Isa. 1:13] but living in accordance with the Lord's [day; cf. Rev. 1:10]—on which also our life arose through him and his death (though some deny it), and by this mystery we received the power to believe, and for this reason we endure so that we may be recognized as disciples of Jesus Christ, our only teacher—2. how shall we be able to live apart from him of whom even the prophets were disciples in the Spirit, him whom they expected as their teacher? And therefore when he came, he whom they righteously awaited raised them from the dead.

9:1–2. Those who walked in ancient or antiquated practices (see on 8:1) came to "newness of hope" (cf. "newness of eternal life," Eph. 19:3; Paul, Rom. 6:4). Like the prophets (Isa. 1:13-14; cf. Barn. 15:8-9), they no longer observed the Sabbath but lived for the Lord's day (Sunday, as in Rev. 1:10; Did. 14:1), on which our life arose (*aneteilen*, probably with an allusion to the sun's rising and hence to Sunday; cf. Rom. 2:2 for a similar play on words). On Sunday, see Volume 1 of this commentary, pp. 174-175. Some deny the reality of his death, and Bauer p. 226 (apparently followed by M. Werner, *Die Entstehung des christlichen Dogmas* [Berne, 1941], 120; *The Formation of Christian Dogma* [New York, 1957], 46) states that they must have denied the resurrection too; but this is highly uncertain. The mystery (i.e., the message of the cross, 1 Cor. 1:18) of the passion leads men to faith, as in 1 Corinthians 1:21 (cf. Eph. 16:2; Trall. 2:1; Justin, *Dialogue* 91 and 131, cited by Lightfoot and Bauer). For Christ as teacher see Ephesians 15:1; but true discipleship comes only through suffering (see on Eph. 3:1). Lightfoot p. 130 claims that "Judaism" and Docetism were combined at Magnesia; it is more likely that Ignatius' reference to those who deny Christ's death is incidental.

For the prophets as Christ's disciples in the Spirit and for their being raised by him, Ignatius apparently relies on "a midrash on Jeremiah" (Daniélou, pp. 260-262), quoted by both Justin (*Dialogue*

10 Let us, then, not be insensible of his goodness, for if he imitated us in our actions we should no longer exist. For this reason we should become his disciples and learn to live in Christian fashion. Whoever is called by any name other than this does not belong to God. 2. Therefore put aside the bad leaven, now antiquated and sour, and turn to the new leaven, which is Jesus Christ [cf. 1 Cor. 5:7]. Be salted with him [cf. Mark 8:15; 9:50], so that none of you may be spoiled, since you will be tested by your odor. 3. It is absurd to talk of Jesus Christ and practice Judaism. For Christianity did not base its faith on Judaism, but Judaism on Christianity, in which "every language" believing in God was "brought together" [Isa. 66:18].

72) and Irenaeus (*Adv. haer.* 3, 20, 4, etc.); something like it was known both to an elder quoted by Irenaeus (*Adv. haer.* 4, 27, 2) and to Marcion (*ibid.*, 1, 27, 3). It read as follows: "The Lord God remembered his dead from Israel [or, the Lord God, the Holy One of Israel, remembered his dead] who slept in the earth of burial, and he descended to them to proclaim his act of salvation to them." Though Ignatius presumably does not know it, his source is Jewish-Christian.

10:1–3.   To continue in Judaism after the coming of Christ and his raising the prophets from the dead is impossible; God's goodness is shown by his still offering men the opportunity to become disciples. Judaism, that is, Jewish Christianity, is not from God.

Therefore the Christian must put aside the "evil leaven, antiquated and soured" ("old leaven" and "leaven of evil" occur in 1 Cor. 5:7-8) and turn to the new leaven, Christ (in Matt. 13:33; Luke 13:21 the kingdom of God is compared with leaven). He must be "salted" with Jesus Christ (cf. Matt. 5:13; Luke 14:34-35; Mark 9:50). Ignatius combines two metaphors traditional among Christians.

One cannot profess Jesus Christ and "Judaize." Historically, Christianity did not develop into faith in Judaism. Instead, Judaism developed into faith in Christianity (by realizing its own true nature; the prophets were disciples of Jesus, chs. 8–9), and now "every tongue" (a remote echo of Isa. 66:18) believing in it has been "gathered together" for God (cf. 2 Clem. 17:4). Ignatius' Old Testament allusion indicates once more that he thinks of the prophets as Christians.

The word *Christianismos* (Christianity), presumably modeled on "Judaism" (2 Macc. 2:21, etc.; 4 Macc. 4:26; Gal. 1:13-14) first occurs in Ignatius' letters (Rom. 3:3; Philad. 6:1; cf. Mart. Polyc. 10:1). It is based, of course, on prior use of the term "Christian" (Acts 11:26; 26:28; 1 Pet. 4:16; Did. 12:4; common in second-century writers) which Ignatius uses five times (Eph. 11:2; Magn. 4:1; Trall. 6:1; Rom. 3:2; Polyc. 7:3).

F. The condition of the Magnesian Christians (11:1–13:2)

11 I say this, my beloved, not because I know that there are any of you who behave thus but because, though less than you, I wish to forewarn you against falling into the snares of vain doctrine and urge you to be fully convinced about the birth and the passion and the resurrection which took place in the time of the rule of Pontius Pilate; for these things were truly and surely done by Jesus Christ, our hope [1 Tim. 1:1], from which may none of you be diverted.

12 May I have joy from you in every respect, if only I am worthy. For since I am in bonds I am not comparable to a single one of you who have been set free. I know that you are not puffed up, for you have Jesus Christ within you. And further, when I praise you I know that you feel shame, as it is written: "The righteous man is his own accuser" [Prov. 18:17].

11:1. As usual, Ignatius insists that his readers are not actually suffering from heresy (Eph 8:1; Trall. 8:1; Philad. 3:1; Smyrn. 4:1). He simply wishes to give them advance warning (Trall. 8:1; Smyrn. 4:1—in each case addressing them as "beloved"), even though he is "less" than they are (another allusion to 1 Cor. 15:9; cf. on Eph. 21:2), and apparently is a very small fish (*pisciculus* in Tertullian, *De baptismo* 1, 3), so that they will not be caught on the fishhooks of error. Instead, they are to retain their full assurance (Philad. inscr.; Smyrn. 1:1; the latter also "kerygmatic") about the birth and the passion and the resurrection (three items, as in Eph. 19:1, but different) which took place "truly and certainly" when Pontius Pilate was governor (cf. Trall. 9:1; Smyrn. 1:2; on his title see J. Vardaman in *Journal of Biblical Literature* 81 [1962], 70-71). Jesus Christ is "our hope" (see on Eph. 21:2); none of the Magnesians is to let himself be turned away from the hope, that is, from him.

12:1. Ignatius asks that he may enjoy the Magnesians in every respect (because of their orthodoxy), provided that he is worthy (enjoy, Eph. 2:2; Magn. 2:1; Rom. 5:2; Polyc. 1:1; 6:2; worthy, Eph. 2:2). Here his feeling of unworthiness is due to the contrast between his being in bonds and their being free (Eph. 12:1; Rom. 4:3); it is the other side of his idea that being in bonds is part of God's plan (Eph. 1:2; 3:1, etc.). They are not "puffed up" (a Pauline expression, especially in 1 Corinthians; cf. Trall. 4:1; 7:1; Polyc. 4:3), for their freedom is due to Jesus Christ, whom they have in themselves (cf. Rom. 6:3). Indeed, they feel shame when he praises them, for according to Proverbs 18:17, "The righteous man is his own accuser." At any rate, such is his own attitude when he is praised (Trall. 4:1-2).

13 Be eager, therefore, to be firmly set in the decrees of the Lord and the apostles so that "in whatever you do you may prosper" [Ps. 1:3]—in flesh and spirit, in faith and love, in the Son and the Father and in the Spirit, at the beginning and at the end, together with your right reverend bishop and that worthily woven spiritual crown, your presbytery, and the godly deacons. 2. Be subject to the bishop and to one another [Eph. 5:21; 1 Pet. 5:5], as Jesus Christ [in the flesh] was subject to the Father and the apostles were subject to Christ [and the Father], so that there may be unity both fleshly and spiritual.

13:1–2. Ignatius ends the main body of his letter with a solemn exhortation to be "firmly set" (the verb here only in his letters, the adverb only in 4:1; and 11:1) in the ordinances of the Lord (cf. Barn. 1:6) and the apostles (cf. Acts 16:4) so that his readers may "prosper" in whatever they do (Ps. 1:3)—in every imaginable way: in flesh and spirit (Trall. inscr.; Rom. inscr.; Philad. 11:2; Smyrn. 1:1; 3:2; Polyc. 5:1), in faith and love (Eph. 1:1; 14:1-2; 20:1; Magn. 1:2; 6:1; Trall. 8:1; Philad. 11:2; Smyrn. inscr.; 16:1; 13:2), in the Son and the Father and the Spirit (only here), at the beginning and the end (Eph. 14:1-2)—together with the "right reverend" (of the Roman church, Rom. inscr.) bishop, the presbytery (a "worthily woven" crown; cf. Paul's words about the Philippians (Phil. 4:1; also 1 Thess. 2:19-20), and the "godly" deacons.

He lists three pairs and one triad: (1) flesh/spirit (Magn. 1:2; Trall. inscr.; Rom. inscr.; Smyrn. 1:1; cf. 13:2); (2) faith/love (Eph. 1:1; 14:1-2; 20:1; Magn. 1:2; Trall. 8:1; Smyrn. inscr.; 13:2); (3) Son/Father (Rom. inscr.; Magn. 1:2; 8:2)/Spirit; (4) beginning/end (Eph. 14:1). The passage is evidently an expansion of Magn. 1:2, where we find flesh/spirit, faith/love, and Jesus/Father. (In Eph. 14:1 faith/love equals beginning/end). To Son/Father, Ignatius adds Spirit but does not or cannot develop the theme. For another example of such expansion see Philadelphians 11:2, where we find flesh/*soul*/spirit and faith/love/*harmony* (cf. faith/love/endurance, Tit. 2:2; 1 Tim. 6:11).

The ordinances he has in mind involve not only being subject to one another, as in Ephesians 5:21 and 1 Peter 5:5, but also being subject to the bishop ("presbyters" in 1 Pet. 5:5)—as Jesus Christ was subject to the Father (cf. Trall. 2:1; John 5:19, 30; 8:28-29; 10:30) and the apostles were subject both to Christ and to the Father (1 Clem. 42:1)—or as the Church is subject to Christ (Eph. 5:24) and is united to him both in flesh and in spirit (Eph. 5:30-32). The ordinances are thus primarily Pauline but may also be Petrine; compare Ignatius' mention of the commands of Peter and Paul (Rom 4:3).

G. Summary and final greeting (14:1–15:1)

14 Since I know that you are full of God I have exhorted you briefly. Remember me in your prayers so that I may attain to God, and remember the church in Syria, from which I am not worthy to be called [1 Cor. 15:9]. For I need your united prayer in God and your love so that the church in Syria may be judged worthy of being refreshed with dew from your church.

15 The Ephesians salute you from Smyrna, from which I am writing you. They are present for God's glory and like you have refreshed me in every way, along with Polycarp, bishop of the Smyrnaeans. The other churches also greet you in honor of Jesus Christ. Farewell in the harmony of God. May you possess an undivided spirit—which is Jesus Christ.

14:1–15:1. All the Ignatian letters follow a relatively fixed pattern toward the end, although not all the elements are always included. Magnesians contains all of them: (1) a statement summarizing what Ignatius has done ("I have exhorted you briefly"; cf. Eph. 21:1); (2) a request for their remembering him in their prayers (Eph. 21:1) or praying for him (Rom. 8:3; cf. Smyrn. 11:1), as well as for the church in Syria (Eph. 21:2; Trall. 13:1; Rom. 9:1; in the later letters he speaks of the consequences of their previous prayer for the church at Antioch (Philad. 10:1; Smyrn. 11:1; Polyc. 7:1), along with a reference to himself as the "least" of the Syrian Christians (Eph. 21:2; Trall. 13:1; Rom. 9:2; Smyrn. 11:1, but not Philadelphians or Polycarp); (3) greetings from Ignatius and/or other Christians to churches or individuals (Trall. 13:1; Rom. 9:3, Philad. 11:2; Smyrn. 12–13; Polyc. 8:2-3; but not Ephesians); and (4) in every letter a final farewell.

In 14:1 Ignatius boldly tells his readers that they are "full of God" (cf. Eph. 15:3; Magn. 12:1; Rom. 6:3; pagan parallels in Bauer p. 230), and asks for their prayer, united with love in God, so that the Syrian church may be "refreshed with dew" (figurative as in Deut. 32:2; Prov. 19:12; see Bauer p. 230).

The Ephesians send their greetings (15:1) from Smyrna; like the Magnesians (cf. Eph. 2:1) and Polycarp of Smyrna (note that Polycarp must be identified for the Magnesians) they have "refreshed" Ignatius (see on Eph. 2:1). Ignatius' final farewell, as in all his letters, is accompanied by a brief word relating it to God's action. Here he mentions "harmony" (Eph. 4:1-2; 13:1; Magn. 6:1; later only in Trallians and Philadelphians) and an undivided spirit, to be identified with Jesus Christ (cf. Eph. 3:2; 17:2; Magn. 7:1; 11:1; Smyrn. 4:1; 10:2).

TRALLIANS

OUTLINE

Salutation
A. The office of the bishop (1:1–3:2)
B. Ignatius' bonds and his knowledge (3:3–5:2)
C. Avoid heresy and heretics (6:1–8:2)
D. Christ's death and resurrection (9:1–11:2)
E. Final greetings (12:1–13:3)

Trallians

Salutation

Ignatius, also called Theophorus, to the holy church at Tralles in Asia—beloved by God the Father of Jesus Christ, elect and worthy of God, at peace in flesh and spirit through the passion of Jesus Christ our hope [1 Tim. 1:1] through his resurrection —which I salute in the fullness after the apostolic pattern and bid abundant greeting.

A. The office of the bishop (1:1–3:2)

1 I know that you have understanding which is blameless and unwavering in endurance, not habitual but innate, as Polybius

---

Salutation. The unique features about the Trallian church, according to this passage, are that it is loved by God (also Rom. inscr.), holy, and at peace (this may mean that Ignatius' remarks about the Docetic heresy are based on the Smyrnaean situation). Ignatius greets the church "after the apostolic fashion"; this means that as at the beginning of Ephesians he imitates the Pauline Ephesians, and in Smyrnaeans imitates 1 Corinthians, so here he is imitating Colossians.

at peace . . . through the passion	Col. 1:20, having made peace through the blood of his cross
Christ our hope	1:27, Christ, . . . the hope of glory
salute in the fullness	1:19, in him all the fullness

Conceivably Ignatius imitates Colossians because he believes that the Trallian situation resembles that at Colossae; but this is most uncertain.

The adjective "holy" is not often used of the early Christian churches; but it occurs in reference to the Church as a whole in Hermas, Vis. 1, 1, 6; 1, 3, 4; 4, 1, 3 (cf. also Did. 10:5). For "peace" see on Ephesians 13:2; for "our hope," on Ephesians 21:2.

On the outline of this letter see J. Moffatt, "An Approach to Ignatius," *Harvard Theological Review* 29 (1936), 1-38, especially 25-31.

1:1–2. As in other letters (Magnesians, Philadelphians, Smyrnaeans), Ignatius begins with a *captatio benevolentiae*, a statement lauding

your bishop informed me when he was with me at Smyrna by the will of God and Jesus Christ, and he so warmly congratulated me—a prisoner in Christ Jesus—that I saw your whole congregation in him. 2. I received your godly love through him and gave God glory because I found you to be (as I knew you were) imitators of God.

2 For when you subject yourselves to the bishop as to Jesus Christ, you appear to me to be living not in human fashion but like Jesus Christ, who died for us so that by believing in his death you might escape dying. 2. Therefore it is necessary that, as is actually the case, you do nothing apart from the bishop, but be subject also to the presbytery as to the apostles of Jesus Christ, our hope [1 Tim. 1:1]; for if we live in him we shall be found in him. 3. Those who are deacons of the mysteries of Jesus Christ [cf. 1 Cor. 4:1] must please all men in every way [1 Cor. 10:33]. For they are not ministers of food and drink but servants [1 Cor. 4:1] of the church of God [cf. 1 Cor. 10:32]; therefore they must guard themselves from accusations as from fire [cf. 1 Cor. 3:15].

---

his readers' character. The Trallians possess a blameless (cf. 13:3 and commentary) understanding (Eph. 20:2), undivided or unhesitating (Magn. 15:1 and commentary) in the endurance characteristic of Christ (Rom 10:3) or of Christians (Eph. 3:1; Smyrn. 12:2; Polyc. 6:2). Their condition is not merely habitual (perhaps against Gnostic claims, cf. W. R. Schoedel in *Journal of Theological Studies* 15 [1964], 308-316) but innate. Ignatius knows this because their bishop visited him "by the will of God and Jesus Christ" (cf. Eph. inscr.) and congratulated him (Eph. 9:2; Philad. 10:1; Smyrn. 11:2) on his being a prisoner for Christ Jesus (cf. Rom. 1:1; Paul, Eph. 3:1; 4:1; Philem. 1, 9), and therefore Ignatius saw the whole congregation in the person of its representative (Eph. 1:3; 2:1; Magn. 2:1; 6:1).

Ignatius received the Trallians' gift of affection (cf. Rom. 4:1), though perhaps they did not actually "refresh" him (see on 12:1); in any event, he found them to be what he already knew they were: imitators of God (Eph. 1:1; Paul, Eph. 5:1).

2:1–3. As in Ephesians and Magnesians, Ignatius turns from praise of the community to insistence upon subjection to the bishop "as to Jesus Christ" (only here; subjection to Christ: Paul, Eph. 5:24); such subjection means living not "in human fashion" (cf. 1 Cor. 3:3) but "in accordance with Jesus Christ" (Philad. 3:2), who died for us (cf. Rom. 6:1). Faith in the reality and significance of his death enables Christians to escape death (thus the Eucharistic emphasis of Eph. 20:2 is not "magical").

3 Similarly all are to respect the deacons as Jesus Christ and the bishop as a copy of the Father and the presbyters as the council of God and the band of the apostles. For apart from these no group can be called a church. 2. I am convinced that you accept this. For I have received an embodiment of your love, and have it with me, in your bishop, whose demeanor is a great lesson and whose gentleness is his power. I think that even the godless revere him.

B. Ignatius' bonds and his knowledge (3:3–5:2)

3. I love you and therefore spare you [1 Cor 7:28], though I could

---

The Trallians must—as they do (see on Eph. 8:1)—do nothing apart from the bishop (see on Magn. 4:1); they must also be subject to the presbytery (Eph. 2:2; Magn. 2:1; Polyc. 6:1) as to the apostles (Magn. 6:1; Trall. 3:1; Philad. 5:1; Smyrn. 8:1) of Jesus Christ our hope (see on Eph. 21:2). He is our hope in the sense that if we live in him (in unity with the bishop), we shall be found in him (cf. 2 Tim. 2:11-13, a "faithful saying").

Ignatius speaks of the deacons' duties, not of the respect due them (this note comes in 3:1). Their function is to be ministers of the mysteries of Jesus Christ and servants of the Church of God; here Ignatius is obviously paraphrasing Paul's words about himself: "Let a man consider us as servants of Christ and stewards of the mysteries of God" (1 Cor. 4:1), as he is when he says that the deacons must "please all in every way" (1 Cor. 10:33). Paul's mysteries are eschatological (see also Eph. 19:1; Magn. 9:1), but it would appear, from Ignatius' statement that the deacons are not "ministers of food and drink," that these mysteries are also sacramental; for "deacons" as "serving tables" see Acts 6:1-6. According to 1 Timothy 3:9, they "must hold the mystery of the faith with a pure conscience"; they are also to serve without reproach (3:10).

3:1–2. Since the deacons are entrusted with the mysteries of Jesus Christ (2:3), they are to be respected as Jesus Christ (cf. Gal. 4:14); they are copies of him, as the bishop is of the Father, and as the presbyters correspond to the "council" or "Sanhedrin" of God ("council of the apostles," Magn. 6:1), equivalent to the "band" of the apostles. There is no Church apart from these orders of ministers.

As often, Ignatius expresses his confidence that what he is recommending is actually being enacted. The ground for his confidence is the presence of the Trallian bishop Polybius (1:1-2), the "embodiment" (originally Latin, *exemplarium*) of their love. His behavior is a great lesson; his gentleness is his power (for the combination of these words see 1 Cor. 4:19-21; for the thought, 2 Cor. 12:9-10). Even the "godless" (perhaps here, as in ch. 10, the heterodox) respect him.

3:3. Ignatius is "sparing" (cf. 1 Cor. 7:28) the Trallians be-

write more sharply on his behalf. I decided not to do so, however, lest though actually a convict, I should give orders to you as if I were an apostle.

4 I have many thoughts in God, but I take my own measure lest I perish through boasting [cf. 2 Cor. 10:13-15]. For it is really much better for me to be fearful and not to pay attention to those who puff me up. For those who speak to me afflict me. 2. I desire to suffer, but I do not know if I am worthy. To many my zeal is not apparent, but it fights all the more against me. I need gentleness, by which the prince of this age is destroyed.

5 Can I not write heavenly things to you? But I fear that I may do harm to "you who are infants" [1 Cor 3:1]. You must pardon me, lest you be choked by what you cannot swallow.

---

cause of his love for them (the idea of 1 Cor. 4:14-21). He could write more sharply in defense of the bishop—who apparently is not completely in control of his church. But a convict cannot give orders as an apostle could (cf. Rom. 4:3; also Eph. 3:1).

4:1–2. Ignatius' "many thoughts in God" (cf. Paul, Phil. 2:5), characteristic of one on his way to perfection (Phil. 3:15; Smyrn. 11:3) cannot be fully revealed to the Trallians (5:1). He does not wish to "think lofty thoughts" (Paul, Rom. 11:20) or to think more highly of himself than he ought to think; instead, he will think in relation to self-control and the "measure" of faith (Paul, Rom. 12:3; see also 2 Cor. 10:13-15). He does not want to perish because of his boasting (cf. Polyc. 5:2; also Eph. 17:2, based on 1 Corinthians 1:18). For "puffing up" see Magnesians 12:1; Trall. 7:1; Smyrn. 6:1; Polyc. 4:3; the word is a Pauline favorite in 1 Corinthians. For fearing rather than thinking lofty thoughts see Paul, Romans 12:3. Those who wrongly praise Ignatius "scourge" him.

Ignatius does desire to suffer, but he does not know whether he is worthy or not (see Introduction). What is not evident to the many is either the jealousy of the devil (Lightfoot p. 162, cf. Rom. 5:3) or his own burning zeal for martyrdom and reaching God (Bauer p. 234). Either interpretation is possible; it may be that Ignatius' zeal could be the means through which the devil works—as the end of his statement suggests. The "prince of this age" is "demolished" (cf. Eph. 19:3) when Ignatius not only suffers but obtains the gentleness which is power (Trall. 3:2).

5:1–2. Now that Ignatius has mentioned "the prince of this age" for the first time in this letter, he imitates the language of Paul

2. For though I am in bonds and can know heavenly things such as the angelic locations and the archontic conjunctions, visible and invisible [cf. Col. 1:16], for all that I am not already a disciple. For many things are lacking to us so that we may not lack God.

C. Avoid heresy and heretics (6:1–8:2)

6 I exhort you therefore—not I but the love of Jesus Christ [cf. 1 Cor. 15:10]—use only Christian food and abstain from every

---

(1 Cor. 3:1-3) and of John (3:12) to indicate that if he wished, he could discuss "heavenly" matters more fully; he has spiritual insight because he is a prospective martyr (Schlier p. 140; cf. the vision of Stephen in Acts 7:56), but "not because of this" (1 Cor. 4:4; also alluded to in Rom. 5:1) has he become a disciple, for discipleship involves following the Lord's example to the end (Corwin 227-235). What we lack in order not to lack God is the full complement of suffering (cf. Col. 1:24-25).

The kind of knowledge which the Trallians might value was related to "angelic locations" (the word *topothesia* is astrological, usually referring to the zodiac; Clement of Alexandria even uses the word *angelothesia*, *Str.* 7, 9, 3; *Eclogae propheticae* 57, 5) and "archontic conjunctions." The word "archontic" reminds us of (1) the devil as the "prince (archon) of this age," (2) Ignatius' mention of angels and archons visible and invisible (Smyrn. 6:1), and (3) the seven "archontic angels" of the Ophite system as described by Celsus and Origen (Origen, *Contra Celsum* 6, 27-35; cf. H. Chadwick, *Origen Contra Celsum* [Cambridge, 1953], 342). It is possible that Ignatius has specific Gnostic knowledge in mind, but it is also possible that he is reflecting what may be called the ingredients of Gnosticism—like those to which Paul alludes in Colossians; and the phrase "visible and invisible" may come from Colossians 1:16.

Not all Christians "are able to receive" (Matt. 19:11) such doctrines (cf. on Smyrn. 6:1). Ignatius does not encourage speculation about angels (cf. Col. 2:18), and his own ideas about them are relatively fixed; note that both here and in Smyrnaeans 6:1 he mentions "heavenly beings," "angels," and "rulers visible and invisible."

6:1–2. Ignatius' exhortations are usually based on something his readers might be expected to know (Rom. 4:1, a proverb; Philad. 8:2, a Pauline phrase [Phil. 2:3]; Eph. 3:2, Trall. 12:2, Christian concord); here his *point d'appui* may be Eucharistic (cf. Rom. 7:3) but is more probably based on 1 Corinthians 3:1 (cf. Trall. 5:1). Primarily, however, he is thinking not so much of "Christian food" as such as of the

strange plant, which is heresy. 2. For they mingle Jesus Christ with themselves, feigning faith, providing something like a deadly drug with honeyed wine, which the ignorant man gladly takes with pleasure; and therein is death.

7 Be on guard against such men. This will be the case for you if you are not puffed up but are inseparable from the God Jesus Christ and the bishop and the ordinances of the apostles. 2. He who is within the sanctuary is pure; he who is outside the sanctuary is not pure—that is, whoever does anything apart from the bishop and the presbytery and the deacons is not pure in conscience.

---

alien, poisonous weed—presumably planted by the devil (Eph. 10:3), not by the Father (Philad. 3:1)—which, he says, is "heresy." This word originally referred to schism rather than heresy (cf. 1 Cor. 11:19), but heresy is probably involved at this point (cf. Trall. 9–11; against Bauer p. 235; see on Eph. 6:2). He takes his exhortation so seriously that he imitates Paul's words in 1 Corinthians 15:10 ("not I, but the grace of God") to say "not I but the love of Jesus Christ" (cf. Philad. 5:1).

From the "heresy" in general he turns to heretics (cf. Tit. 3:10) in particular, using a rather common simile (cf. *Journal of Biblical Literature* 63 [1944], 370-371) in order to compare them with honeyed wine and their doctrine with a deadly poison. As Bauer p. 235 points out, the simile is usually (and in medicine always) employed to illustrate the "sugar-coating" of a bitter pill. Ignatius' meaning, however, is perfectly clear. For other medical images see Eph. 7:2; 20:2; Polyc. 2:1. As H. Riesenfeld points out (*Texte und Untersuchungen* 79 [1961], 317), they are "tools of speech which he might have acquired at school." The expression "deadly drug" suggests that we should not take too literally the description of the Eucharist as the drug or medicine of immortality in Ephesians 20:2.

7:1–2. In warning here against heretics, Ignatius uses the Attic form of the verb (*phylattesthe*); elsewhere he uses the Koiné form *phylassesthai* (Eph. 2:1, Trall. 2:3)—an instance of his lack of concern for precise consistency. The Trallians, like the Magnesians (12:1) and slaves at Smyrna (Polyc. 4:3) are not to be puffed up (a word, common in 1 Corinthians, which Paul uses of partisan rivalry in 1 Cor. 4:6); instead, they are to observe the Christian hierarchy or chain of command.

To be within the sanctuary (with the Eucharistic bread of God and the bishop, Eph. 5:2) is to be pure, not ritually but in conscience (cf. 1 Tim. 3:9; 2 Tim. 1:3).

8 It is not that I know of anything of the sort among you, but I warn you in advance because you are dear to me and I foresee the snares of the devil. Therefore you must take on gentleness and renew yourselves in faith, the Lord's flesh, and in love, the blood of Jesus Christ. 2. None of you is to bear a grudge against his neighbor. Give no opportunity to the Gentiles, lest the congregation of God be blasphemed through a few fools. For "woe to him through whom my Name is vainly blasphemed among any" [cf. Isa. 52:5].

8:1–2. Does Ignatius protest too much? He has also told the Magnesians (Magn. 11) that his warning is either hypothetical or prophetic. One can, of course, suspect that when he says something like this he does so only because it is not true (cf. also Philad. 7:2); but suspicion rarely leads to conclusive proof, at least in the absence of evidence.

The snares of the prince of this age are mentioned in Philadelphians 6:2; they include whatever takes Christians away from Christ. The remedy for them consists of (1) suffering with gentleness (cf. 1 Tim. 6:11) and (2) renewal in faith and love (on these modes of Christian existence see Eph. 1:1). It is especially striking that Ignatius says of faith that it is the flesh of the Lord, of love that it is the blood of Jesus Christ. In Romans 7:3 he says that the blood of Jesus Christ is imperishable love, and in Philadelphians 5:1 he compares the gospel with the flesh of Jesus. Bauer p. 236 speaks of the bold identification which Ignatius makes but does not explain it (similarly p. 252).

In dealing with Philadelphians 5:1, however (Bauer p. 258), points out that Ignatius identifies the gospel with (the flesh of) Jesus; therefore, to believe in the gospel means to believe in Jesus and faith can be regarded as analogous to his flesh. In order to understand Trallians 8 we must consider the fact that already in the Pauline epistles "the blood of Christ" is a traditional formula (1 Cor. 10:16; 11:25, 27) and that the teaching about it can be presupposed (Rom. 3:25; 5:9; Eph. 1:7; 2:13; Col. 1:20; see F. Grandchamp in *Revue de théologie et de philosophie* 11 [1961], 262-271). Ignatius builds on this tradition, especially as developed in such a letter as the Pauline Ephesians, where a mention of Christ's blood is followed by a description of him as "our peace" (Eph. 2:13-14). This is to say that the blood of Christ (his death) produced (and therefore was) peace for us. Similarly his blood produced, and therefore implies, love —and "eternal and lasting joy" (Philad. inscr.). For Ignatius the blood of Christ is supremely important (see also Philad. 4:1; Smyrn. 1:1; 6:1; 12:2; and, for the "blood of God," Eph. 1:1). On Christ's blood as a ransom see M. E. Boismard in *Revue biblique* 69 (1962), 446 f.

D. Christ's death and resurrection (9:1–11:2)

9 Be deaf, then, when anyone speaks to you apart from Jesus Christ, who was of the family of David, who was of Mary, who was truly born, ate and drank, was truly persecuted under Pontius Pilate, was truly crucified and died, while heavenly, earthly, and subterranean beings looked on. 2. He was also truly raised from the dead, when his Father raised him up, as in similar fashion his Father will raise up in Christ Jesus us who believe him—without whom we have no true life.

10 But if, as some godless men—that is, unbelievers—say, his suffering was only apparent (they are the apparent ones), why am I in bonds, why do I pray to fight wild beasts? [1 Cor. 15:32.] Then I die in vain. Then I lie about the Lord [1 Cor. 15:15-16].

Ignatius uses the word "neighbor" only twice (cf. Magn. 6:2), both times implicitly in regard to "love of neighbor." The expressions "to have something against" and "to give occasion" both occur in 2 Corinthians 5:12. Ignatius has in mind the point made in 2 Clement 13: Christians must practice what they preach—with a similar quotation from something like Isaiah 52:5 (cf. Polycarp, Phil. 10:3).

9:1–2. Heretics are to be avoided (Tit. 3:10) and disregarded, since they do not teach the true faith, which Ignatius briefly sets forth in a semicredal passage. Jesus Christ was "of the family of David," directly "of Mary" (see on Eph. 18:2); he was born, ate and drank (cf. Smyrn. 3:3; Matt. 11:19; Luke 7:34), was persecuted under Pontius Pilate (cf. 1 Tim. 6:13), was crucified, and died. All these items prove his reality as a human being, as does Ignatius' reference to the witnesses to his crucifixion (cf. Phil. 2:10 for a similar reference based on Isa. 45:23). For similar statements see Ephesians 18:2 and Smyrnaeans 1:1-2.

Jesus Christ was truly raised and his resurrection was an anticipation of that of Christians (1 Cor. 15:12-20; Rom. 8:11). Apart from him they have no true life; he is their life (Smyrn. 4:1; John 11:25-26; 14:6; Col. 3:4).

10:1. The "godless" (3:2) or "unbelievers" (Magn. 5:2; Smyrn. 2:1; cf. 5:3)—apparently heretics, to judge from what they say—claim that Christ Jesus seemed to suffer, presumably because of their views of his deity (see on Polyc. 3:2). As in Smyrnaeans 2:1, Ignatius says that they themselves merely seem to exist, since they have no true life (Trall. 9:1) or salvation. He proceeds to imitate Paul's arguments about the resurrection in 1 Corinthians 15:32 (fighting wild beasts) and 1 Corinthians 15:15-16 (false witness against God). Note

11 Flee from the wicked offshoots which bear deadly fruit; if a man tastes them he soon dies [cf. John 6:49]. These are not the planting of the Father [Matt. 15:13]. 2. For if they were, they would appear as branches of the cross and their fruit would be imperishable. By the cross through his passion he calls upon you who are his members. The head cannot be begotten apart from the members, since God promises union—himself.

E. Final greetings (12:1–13:3)

12 I salute you from Smyrna together with the churches of God which are present with me, men who in every respect have refreshed me in flesh and spirit. 2. My bonds exhort you, bonds which I bear for Jesus Christ, praying that I may reach God: continue in your harmony and in prayer with one another. It is fitting for each of you, especially the presbyters, to refresh the bishop, to the honor of the Father, Jesus Christ, and the

---

that here Ignatius' model is Paul, while in Smyrnaeans 2–3 it is Peter (mentioned together in Rom. 4:3).

11:1–2. Elsewhere Ignatius urges his readers to "flee from" wicked arts (Philad. 6:2; Polyc. 5:1) or division (Philad. 2:1; 7:2) and to avoid wicked weeds not planted by the Father (Philad. 3:1 and commentary). He has already told the Trallians (6:1) that such plants are poisonous. Perhaps his mention of tasting and dying has Eucharistic overtones (cf. John 6:49; Eph. 20:2), but this is uncertain.

Ignatius' main concern is with the contrast between the cross as the tree of life planted by the Father (cf. Smyrn. 1:2), with branches consisting of true Christians (cf. Paul, Rom. 11:16-21; also the disciples as fruit-bearing branches, John 15:1-6). On the cross as the tree of life see K. Goetz in *Zeitschrift für die neutestamentliche Wissenschaft* 20 (1921), 93; J. Daniélou, *Theologie du Judéo-Christianisme* (Tournai, 1958), 289-316; *Primitive Christian Symbols* (Baltimore, 1964), 36-41. As usual, Ignatius' metaphor changes—from branches to members of the body (as in Smyrn. 1:2): *through* the cross *by* the passion Christ calls his members. Compare Ephesians 9:1: the cross is "the crane of Jesus Christ." For the inseparability of the members from the head see Colossians 2:19 and Ephesians 4:15-16. Faith and love joined together in unity are God, in Ignatius' view (Eph. 14:1).

12:1–3. Ignatius draws the attention of the Trallians to the "refreshment," material and spiritual, which other churches have provided for him at Smyrna (cf. Eph. 2:1; Magn. 15:1; Smyrn. 9:2; 12:1). These churches included those of Ephesus, Smyrna, and Magnesia, but not, it would appear, either Tralles or Philadelphia.

apostles. 3. I pray you to hear me in love so that I may not be a
witness against you as I write. And pray also for me, that I may
be judged worthy of the lot which I am set to obtain, "lest I be
found a castaway" [1 Cor. 9:27].

13 The love of the Smyrnaeans and the Ephesians salutes you.
Remember in your prayers the church in Syria, whence I am

Only here do Ignatius' bonds exhort anyone (elsewhere "I exhort"),
but he can speak vividly of them as "spiritual pearls" (Eph. 11:2) and
as a sacrificial offering on behalf of his readers (Smyrn. 10:2; Polyc.
2:3); "living water" can speak in him (Rom. 7:2); therefore this
product of his imagination is not surprising (cf. Eph. 19:1-3 and commentary). They provide the means by which he can "reach God"
(see on Eph. 12:2). The exhortation is that of Ephesians 3:2—to
harmony (here depicted as already achieved, see on Eph. 8:1), and
to common prayer (on the importance of common prayer see Eph.
5:2; Magn. 7:1; 14:1; another exhortation to prayer, Polyc. 1:3).
Ignatius' mention of harmony, and of the "refreshment" given him by
other churches, leads him back to the Trallians' duty to "refresh"
or "support" their own bishop (cf. 3:2-3). On "it is fitting" see on
Ephesians 2:2. To refresh him is to honor the Father, whom he represents (he who honors the bishop has been honored by God, Smyrn.
9:1); it is to honor Jesus Christ, who did nothing apart from the
Father (Magn. 7:1); and when the presbyters refresh the bishop, they
are analogously imitating the apostles, whom they represent (cf. on
Magn. 6:1).
Ignatius asks the Trallians to hear him so that his letter will not
give his testimony against them; for the meaning of this expression
see on Philadelphians 6:3. He asks (*euchomai* occurs in his letters
only in the first person singular); they are to pray (*proseuchomai* only
in the second person plural) for him and thus express and, indeed,
make effective their love in God's mercy so that he may be deemed
worthy (cf. Eph. 20:1; Magn. 1:2) to obtain the "lot" of martyrdom
(cf. Rom. 1:2; Philad. 5:1) and not "be found a castaway" (1 Cor.
9:27).
13:1–3.   Greetings are sent to the Trallians by the churches to
which Ignatius feels himself to be most closely related (cf. Magn.
15:1) or rather by their "love" (so the love of certain churches, Rom.
9:3, and of the brothers at Troas, Philad. 11:2; Smyrn. 12:1). As in
Ephesians 21:2, Magnesians 14:1, and Romans 9:1, Ignatius asks for
prayers for the church in Syria and speaks of his own unworthiness
to be called a Syrian Christian (see on Eph. 21:2).
With the ordinary expression "farewell" Ignatius combines, as
usual, a specifically Christian note ("in Jesus Christ" here as in Eph.
21:2; Philad. 11:2). The Trallians are to be subject to the bishop as

not worthy to be named, since I am the least of them [1 Cor. 15:8-9]. 2. Farewell in Jesus Christ, and be subject to the bishop as to the commandment and likewise to the presbytery. And each of you must love one another with undivided heart. 3. My spirit is consecrated for you not only now but also when I attain to God. For I am still in danger, but the Father is faithful in Jesus Christ to fulfill my petition and yours; may you be found blameless in him.

---

to the commandment (cf. Smyrn. 8:1) and also to the presbytery (similar statements in Eph. 2:2; Magn. 2:1; Polyc. 6:1). The commandment may be the Johannine "love one another," to which Ignatius immediately turns (John 13:34; 15:12); this is love "with undivided heart" (Philad. 6:2).

The likelihood that Ignatius is following Johannine themes is increased by his statement about the sacrificial consecration of his spirit (cf. John 17:19; Eph. 8:1; Smyrn. 10:2) for them not only when he writes but also when he attains to God, that is, through martyrdom; compare John 15:13 (the greatest love is to lay down one's life) and 1 John 3:16 ("we too should lay down our lives for the brothers"). Note also John 13:35: "By this all men will know that you are my disciples, if you have love for one another"; this resembles Ignatius' idea of becoming a disciple through sacrificial love (Eph. 1:2; Magn. 9:1; Rom. 4:2; 5:3). The "danger" in which Ignatius stands is the danger of not being a martyr (see Eph. 12:1); but the faithful (trustworthy) Father will provide a way of enduring temptation (1 Cor. 10:13). May the Trallians be found blameless in Jesus Christ (cf. 1 Cor. 1:8-9; Phil. 2:15; Col. 1:22; Eph. 1:4; 5:27).

ROMANS

OUTLINE

Salutation
A. Ignatius' petition (1:1–3:3)
B. Ignatius' sacrifice (4:1–5:3)
C. Ignatius' temptations (6:1–7:2a)
D. Union with Christ (7:2b–8:3)
E. Final greetings (9:1–10:3)

Romans

Salutation

Ignatius, also called Theophorus, to her who has obtained mercy by the greatness of the Father Most High and of Jesus Christ his only Son, to the church beloved and enlightened by the will of him who willed all things that exist, in accordance with the love of Jesus Christ our God—the church which presides in the place of the country of the Romans, worthy of God, worthy of honor, worthy of blessing, worthy of praise, worthy of success, worthy of sanctification, and pre-eminent in love, named after Christ, named after the Father; which I salute in the name of Jesus Christ, Son of the Father—to those who are united in flesh and spirit to every commandment of his, filled with God's grace without wavering, and filtered clean of every alien stain: abundant greeting in blamelessness in Jesus Christ our God.

Salutation. The inscription of the Romans letter consists of three parts: (1) a rather conventional introduction (God's mercy is also mentioned in the inscriptions to Philadelphians and Smyrnaeans; for "beloved" cf. Trallians and Smyrnaeans) which ends with "Jesus Christ our God"; (2) a rhetorical but explicit description of the Roman church, greeted "in the name of Jesus Christ, Son of the Father"; and (3) the greeting itself, addressed to the heresy-free Roman Christians "in Jesus Christ our God." The second section is especially important because it states that the Roman church "presides (as the bishop and other ministers do in Magn. 6:1-2) in the place of the country of the Romans" (apparently a reference to the city and its environs). This church is also pre-eminent in love, probably the works of love mentioned in 1 Clement 55:2 and by Dionysius of Corinth (Eusebius, *H.E.* 4, 23, 10). There is apparently no reference here to a universal Roman primacy (against O. Perler in *Divus Thomas* 22 [1944], 413-451; he lays emphasis on "faith and love" but this occurs again in Smyrn. inscr.). From the third section we learn that the Romans are "filled with God's grace" (as the Smyrnaeans lack no gift and are filled with faith and love) "without wavering" (like the Philadel-

85

A. Ignatius' petition (1:1–3:3)

1 Since by praying to God I have attained the sight of your
faces, worthy of God, so that I have obtained more than I asked
—for as a prisoner in Christ Jesus [cf. Eph. 3:1] I hope to greet
you, if it be God's will that I be judged worthy to the end. . . .
2. For the beginning has been well ordered, if only I may
attain grace to come unhindered to my lot. For I fear your love,
lest it itself harm me. For it is easy for you to do what you wish,
but it is difficult for me to reach God if you do not spare me.

---

phians; cf. also Magn. 15:1, Trall. 1:1) and have been "filtered clean"
(cf. Philad. 3:1) of every alien stain or color. J. B. Bauer (*Divus
Thomas* 41 [1963], 292-293) well compares these words with the
Gospel of Philip, p. 109, 12-20, and 111, 25-30, where baptism is compared with being colored white by God the dyer. For "Jesus Christ
our God" see Introduction.

1:1–2. Ignatius' prayer (usually directed toward martyrdom) has
obtained for him (as he hopes the Ephesians' prayer will do, Eph.
1:2) the privilege of seeing the Romans' faces—worthy of God (cf.
Trall. inscr.; Rom. inscr.; also Magn. 2:1; Smyrn. 12:2). He will have
obtained more than he asked for, since he has asked for only the privilege of being a martyr (of being, like Paul [Eph. 3:1], a prisoner
for Christ Jesus), but will also see them, if it is God's will (cf. Paul,
Rom. 1:10) that he be found worthy (cf. Eph. 21:2) to the end
(Eph. 14:2, Rom. 10:3). Syntactically, his sentence is incomplete
(cf. Magn. 2:1).

Everything has an end (Magn. 5:1) and the end of life is death; a
martyr's death means "reaching God" by divine grace—provided that
the Romans do not intervene. A well-arranged beginning should lead
to the Christian's true "lot" (Trall. 12:3; Philad. 5:1; Eph. 11:2)—
by divine grace (cf. 1 Pet. 2:20). Why is Ignatius afraid of the
Romans' love? He thinks that they may prevent his martyrdom by
somehow "pleasing men" or speaking (with a petition of some sort)
on his behalf (2:1). Perhaps a clue as to what he expects, or fears,
they may do is given in 3:1: "you have taught others"—a probable
allusion not only to 1 Peter but also to 1 Clement. Then his urging
that "what you taught in your instructions" may stand fast would
refer to the picture of the endurance of Jesus (1 Pet. 2:20-25; 1
Clem. 16) and of the apostles and other Christians (1 Clem. 5–6),
while his fear of their love would be based on the Roman Christians'
practice of delivering "themselves to bondage in order to ransom
others" (1 Clem. 55:2). This seems more likely than the hypothesis
that highly placed Roman Christians could get a condemned Christian freed by using influence at court.

2 I wish you not to please men but to please God [cf. 1 Thess. 2: 4; 4:1], as you do please him [cf. 1 Thess. 4:1]. For I shall never have such an opportunity for attaining to God, nor do you, if you keep silent, have any better deed for which to be credited. For if you are silent about me, I am a word of God; but if you love my flesh, I shall again be only a voice. 2. Grant me nothing more than to be poured forth to God while an altar is still ready, so that forming a chorus in love you may sing to the Father in Christ Jesus that God has judged the bishop of Syria worthy to be found at the west [setting] after sending him across from the

---

2:1-2. If the Romans please God rather than men (an echo of 1 Thess. 2:4)—as indeed they do (a typically Ignatian expression; cf. 1 Thess. 4:1)—they will be silent about Ignatius, that is, not try to prevent his martyrdom. He will never have a better occasion for "reaching God" (see on Eph. 10:1; for such an "occasion" see Polyc. 2:3); they can be engaged in no better work (or, possibly, with reference to the altar about to be mentioned, their names can be figuratively inscribed in relation to no better work). Their silence will permit Ignatius to be a "word of God"; their speech (loving his flesh but not his spirit) will make him, again, nothing but a "voice." In view of the fact that Ignatius certainly knows the Matthaean story of Jesus' baptism by John (Smyrn. 1:1), and probably knows the Gospel of John, it seems likely that his contrast between "word" and "voice" is based on the distinction between Jesus as the "Word" of God (Magn. 8:2) and John, the forerunner, as a "voice" (Matt. 3:3; John 1:23; Heracleon in Origen, *Ioh. comm.* 6, 20). This is to say that Ignatius expects to "reach" not only God but, specifically, Jesus Christ (5:3); he desires not only to imitate his suffering (6:3) but also to suffer with him (Smyrn. 4:2). He has Jesus Christ in himself (Magn. 12:1; Rom. 6:3), and as he dies through him "in relation to his passion" his life is in him (Magn. 5:2).

Like Paul (Phil. 2:17; cf. 2 Tim. 4:6), Ignatius regards himself as a libation poured out to God. The altar (here alone in the letters *thysiastērion* bears this meaning) is still ready; presumably, as Lightfoot p. 201 notes, it is the Flavian amphitheater at Rome. Around this altar, as at a pagan sacrifice, the Roman Christians should sing the sacrificial hymn to the Father. This hymn is one for "evensong," for it expresses thanks for letting Ignatius, sent from the sun's rising, be found at the sun's setting; he will set like the sun, but away from the world toward God, in order to rise toward him. For Rome as the west see also 1 Clem. 5:6-7; also L. Voelkl, " 'Orientierung' im Welt-bild der ersten christlichen Jahrhunderte," *Rivista di archeologia cristiana* 25 (1949), 55-70. In this passage Ignatius refers to himself as "the bishop of Syria" (not "the Syrian bishop," cf. 9:1). It would

east [rising]. It is good to set from the world toward God so that I may rise toward him.

3 You have never envied anyone; you have taught others. But I desire the instructions you have given to stand fast. 2. Only pray that I may have power, both within and without, so that I may not only be called a Christian but be found to be one. For if I am found to be one, I can also be called one, and then can be faithful when I disappear from the world. 3. Nothing that appears is good, for our God Jesus Christ appears all the more clearly because he is in the Father. Christianity is a matter not of persuasiveness [cf. 1 Cor. 2:4] but of greatness when it is hated by the world.

---

therefore appear that he was the metropolitan of Syria as bishop of Antioch; his letters to the various churches and to a bishop suggest that he was not unaccustomed to writing pastoral epistles. This is to say that the see of Antioch was essentially patriarchal at the beginning of the second century as well as toward the end, when we find Serapion of Antioch directing the affairs of the nearby seacoast town of Rhossus (Eusebius, *H.E.* 6, 12, 3-6).

3:1–3. Ignatius' reference to the Roman church as never having envied but having taught others may well reflect his knowledge of 1 Clement, especially since (1) the instructions of 1 Clement were specifically directed against jealousy or envy (63:2), (2) Ignatius goes on to speak of the Romans' instructions, (3) he has just spoken of the bishop of Syria as having come from east to west (like Paul in 1 Clem. 5:6), and (4) he is about to speak of Peter and Paul (4:3; 1 Clem. 5:4-5). Ignatius does not say that hindering his martyrdom would be an expression of envy, but he may think that it would.

He needs the prayers of the Roman church (as he needs the prayers of others, Eph. 1:2; 11:2; 21:1; Magn. 14:1; Philad. 5:1; 8:2; Smyrn. 11:1) so that he can declare himself a Christian (cf. 1 Pet. 4:16) and do so without fear. His inner disposition will be more important than the mere declaration.

Ignatius goes on to compare himself (cf. 4:2) with "our God Jesus Christ," who was not fully recognized during his earthly life (cf. 1 Cor. 2:8; Eph. 19:1) but now being "in the Father" (John 14:11, 20; 17:21) is plainly visible (cf. John 14:9). Christianity is not a matter of persuading others (cf. 1 Cor. 2:4) but of deeds (cf. Eph. 14–15); its greatness (Eph. inscr.; Smyrn. 11:2) is evident when it is "hated by the world" (cf. John 15:18-19; 17:14; 1 John 3:13; also Matt. 10:22, to which there may be an allusion in Rom. 10:3).

B. Ignatius' sacrifice (4:1–5:3)

4 I am writing to all the churches and I command all men: I am voluntarily dying for God if you do not hinder me. I exhort you not to be an "inopportune favor" to me. (Let me be food for the wild beasts, through which I can attain to God. I am the wheat of God and I am ground by the teeth of wild beasts so that I may be found the pure bread of Christ.) 2. Instead, entice the wild beasts so that they may become my tomb and leave no trace of my body, so that when I fall asleep I may not burden anyone. Then I shall be truly a disciple of Jesus Christ, when the world will not see my body at all. Pray to Christ for me that through these means I may be found a sacrifice to God. 3. I do not give you orders as Peter and Paul did. They were apostles; I am a convict. They were free; I am still a slave. But if I suffer I shall be Christ's freedman [1 Cor. 7:22] and in him I shall rise free. Now I am learning in bonds to desire nothing.

4:1–3. The message and command (1 Cor. 7:17) Ignatius is giving to "all the churches" (cf. Polyc. 8:1) is that he is "voluntarily" (cf. 1 Cor. 9:17) dying "for the sake of God" (cf. "for the sake of Christ," 2 Cor. 12:10; Phil. 1:29), if they do not "hinder" him, perhaps as some disciples wanted to "hinder" children from coming to Christ (Matt. 19:14; Mark 10:14; Luke 18:16). They must not provide the proverbial "inopportune favor" (equivalent to hostility, Zenobius, *Paroemiographia* 1, 50). They must let Ignatius become food for the beasts and attain to God (cf. Eph. 1:2; Smyrn. 4:2). At this point he identifies himself with the Eucharistic bread and even, perhaps, with unleavened bread (cf. 1 Cor. 5:7-8; Magn. 10:2); perhaps he will be a "pure" sacrifice like the one mentioned in Malachi 1:11 (Did. 14:1, 3). See H. Riesenfeld in *Texte und Untersuchungen* 77 (1961), 54.

Origen (*Homilies on Leviticus* 7, 5) states that "pure food" means (1) the flesh of Jesus, (2) Peter and Paul and all the apostles, and (3) the disciples of the apostles. "Thus each one, in proportion to his merits or the purity of his senses, is made 'pure food' for his neighbor." This idea may be based on Ignatius' letter, which Origen knew (see on Rom. 7:2, part 2).

The beasts will be his tomb, and the world will no longer see his body—just as the world no longer sees Jesus (John 14:19)—and then he will become a disciple (cf. Eph. 1:2; 3:1; Magn. 9:2; Trall. 5:2). They must pray to (or "supplicate") Christ—the first instance of such prayer—that he may be a sacrifice to God (see Introduction).

Ignatius does not give orders as if he were an apostle (Trall. 3:3;

5 From Syria to Rome I am fighting with wild beasts by land and sea, night and day, bound to ten leopards—that is, a company of soldiers—and when they are treated well they become worse. I become more of a disciple because of their mistreatment of me, "but not by this am I justified" [1 Cor. 4:4]. 2. I would enjoy the beasts that have been prepared for me, and I pray that they may be found prompt for me; I will even coax them to consume me promptly—not as in the cases of some whom they

cf. Eph. 3:1; Paul does give orders, 1 Cor. 7:17 [in all the churches]; 11:34; 16:1; Tit. 1:5), for he is a slave, with only the future reward of freedom (cf. Polyc. 4:3). He is learning to be truly free by desiring nothing (earthly, 2 Clem. 5:6); this is the Cynic-Stoic ideal. For the apostle as free, compare 1 Cor. 9:1; for Christians as the Lord's freedmen, 1 Cor. 7:22.

5:1–3. Ignatius' description of his struggles recalls the form employed by Graeco-Roman kings and generals in describing their accomplishments (on this cf. A. Fridrichsen in *Symbolae Osloenses* 7 [1928], 25-29; 8 [1929], 78-82). Specific parallels to his fighting "from Syria to Rome" occur in two inscriptions printed by W. Dittenberger, *Orientis Graeci Inscriptiones Selectae* (Leipzig, 1903), I, 201, 16 and 199, 30. Compare also Paul, Romans 15:19: "from Jerusalem round about to Illyricum." Similarly the fighting with wild animals; in Appian, *Bellum Civile* 2, 60, 252, Pompey says, "We fight as with wild animals." Ignatius is using the regal-imperial style to describe his exploits. He is in a peculiar situation in relation to the wild animals, however. Here as in Trallians 10:1 (modeled after 1 Cor. 15: 32), the animals are metaphorical; but in Ephesians 1:2 they are real —as in the rest of his letter to the Romans. He is in the kind of situation in which nightmares are on the verge of becoming realities.

The expression "by land and sea, night and day" serves to indicate the completeness of his captivity, as in a somewhat similar Pauline passage (2 Cor. 11:23-27). It has sometimes been suggested that in biblical writings the mention of night before day reflects Semitic influence, but since this is often the case in Greek writers such as Xenophon and the second-century rhetoricians Dio Chrysostom and Aelius Aristides, we may assume that it does not do so here.

Leopards are mentioned by several second-century writers (cf. Lightfoot pp. 212-213). Bauer p. 249 says that "ten men as escort for one seem a little lavish." Perhaps Ignatius was an important prisoner; perhaps there were other prisoners, not Christians, with him.

Elsewhere Ignatius always longs for persons whom he knows (Eph. 2:2; Magn. 2:1; 12:1; Polyc. 1:1; 6:2). Writing to the Romans, whom he does not know personally, he concentrates

were afraid to touch. Even if they are unwilling, I will force them. 3. Indulge me; I know what is to my advantage; now I am beginning to be a disciple. May nothing visible or invisible [cf. Col. 1:16] be jealous of my attaining to Jesus Christ. Fire and cross, packs of wild beasts, cuttings, rendings, crushing of bones, mangling of limbs, grinding of my whole body, wicked torture of the devil—let them come upon me if only I may attain to Jesus Christ.

C. Ignatius' temptations (6:1-7:2a)

6 The ends of the earth and the kingdoms of this age are of no profit to me. It is better for me to die [1 Cor. 9:15] for Jesus Christ than to be king over the ends of the earth. I seek him who

---

his attention upon the wild beasts and prays that they will speedily devour him. He has heard of cases (later examples in Bauer p. 249) in which the animals were afraid to touch their prospective victims. If they are unwilling, he will force them to their task, as the later martyr Germanicus did (Mart. Polyc. 3:1).

Concede this to me, says Ignatius; grant me this favor (similar expressions in 6:2; Trall. 5:1). He uses a compound form of *gnōmē* and the word *sympherei*—an echo of 2 Corinthians 8:10, however faint? He knows what is good for him: to continue on his way to being a disciple (Eph. 1:2; 3:1; Trall. 5:2; Rom. 4:3). Nothing visible or invisible (cf. Trall. 5:2; Smyrn. 6:1) should be envious of his attaining to Jesus Christ (here only; otherwise, to God; but Jesus Christ is God). He is willing for every kind of cruel torture to come upon him if he can so attain. In Smyrnaeans 4:2 he thinks of fire, sword, and wild beasts; with the list given here we may compare the afflictions of those who endure suffering for "the Name" in Hermas, Visions 3, 2, 1: beastings, imprisonments, great tribulations, crosses, wild beasts. A.-G. 764 speaks of "the unbridled imagination of Ignatius," but in view of the fact that most of the tortures he mentions were known in Roman times, "unbridled" is not a good word.

6:1-3. Ignatius' words are based on the Gospel sayings about self-denial and self-sacrifice as contrasted with "gaining the whole world" (Mark 8:34-36 and parallels); he may also have in mind the devil's offering Jesus "the kingdoms of the world" (Matt. 4:8; Luke 4:5), since he has just mentioned the devil (5:3). He would rather die (a verbal parallel to 1 Cor. 9:15) in relation to Christ Jesus (cf. Paul, Rom. 6:3, a baptism into Christ's death, which for Ignatius—cf. Mark 10:38; Luke 12:50—involves suffering). For the contrast between reigning and suffering see 1 Corinthians 4:

died for us; I want him who rose for us. Childbearing is upon me.
2. Indulge me, brothers: do not keep me from living; do not desire me to die. Do not give the world one who wants to belong
to God, nor lead him astray with matter. Let me receive the
pure light; when I arrive there I shall be a man. 3. Let me be
an imitator of the passion of my God. If anyone has him within
himself, he must understand what I want and sympathize
with me, since he knows what drives me on [cf. 2 Cor. 5:14].

7 The prince of this age wants to abduct me and corrupt my
mind set on God. None of you present must help him; instead,
be on my side, that is, God's. Do not speak of Jesus Christ
and desire the world. 2a. No envy must dwell among you. Even
if when I arrive I exhort you, do not obey me; instead, obey what
I am writing you now. I write you while alive but desiring to die.

8-13. Ignatius seeks not earthly glory but Christ, who died and
rose for us (cf. Paul, Rom. 8:34). He is suffering labor pains
(Gal. 4:19) as a mother (the old, dying Ignatius) and as a child
(the new, living Ignatius).

He wants to belong to God, not to the world or to matter;
he wants to receive the "pure light" of God, to be in God's
realm, to become a genuine man—the "new man" of the New
Testament. Similarly in the Gospel of Philip, to receive grace is
to put on perfect light and become perfect light, to grasp the
perfect man and become a perfect man (p. 124, 22-23; cf. p. 124,
1; also Smyrn. 4:2).

He is going to do so by imitating, that is, re-enacting, the "passion of my God." Monophysites naturally quoted these words to
show that Christ suffered as God; Ignatius was not concerned
with exact theological definitions. If anyone—like Ignatius and
like Paul (Gal. 2:20)—has Jesus Christ in himself (Magn. 12:1),
he should understand spiritually (Trall. 5:2; cf. Smyrn. 1:1) what
Ignatius desires and "sympathize with" (a word which also means
"suffer with," cf. 1 Cor. 12:26; Rom. 8:17) him. Ignatius speaks of
suffering with Christ in Smyrnaeans 4:2. Perhaps both meanings are
involved here.

7:1–2a. The prince of this age (see on Eph. 17:1) is eager to
capture Christians (Eph. 17:1; Philad. 6:2) or to oppress them (Magn.
1:2); but Ignatius' purpose or mind is directed toward God (cf. Philad.
1:2). The Romans must help him—and God. They must not speak of
Jesus Christ and want something contrary to him (cf. Magn. 10:3;
though they must speak in relation to, or about, Jesus Christ, Trall.
9:1; Philad. 6:1).

D. Union with Christ (7:2b–8:3)

2b. My desire has been crucified [cf. Gal. 6:14] and in me there is no matter-loving fire; there is water living and speaking in me, saying from within me, "Come to the Father." 3. I take no pleasure in the food of corruption or in the pleasures of this life. I desire the bread of God [John 6:33], which is the flesh of Jesus Christ (who was of the seed of David), and for drink I desire his blood, which is imperishable love.

8 I no longer wish to live in human fashion; and this will take place if you are willing. Desire it, so that you may be desired.

There must be no envy among them (cf. 3:1); therefore when Ignatius reaches Rome they must obey his instructions written now, while he is alive but desires to die, not those which he might give at Rome—half-dead and desiring false life (cf. 6:2), life that is merely human (8:1).

7:2b–8:3. Ignatius though living—in the world of matter—writes of his desire to die (the verb *eraō*, "to love," never occurs in the New Testament, among the Apostolic Fathers only here and in 2:1 and Polyc. 4:3). His *erōs* (earthly or worldly desire) has been crucified. This famous sentence was misunderstood by Origen (*Commentaries on the Song of Songs*, prologue) and Theodore of Studium (PG 99, 1797), who thought he was referring to Christ (cf. A. Nygren, *Agape and Eros* [London, 1953], 387-392). A Christian writer could use *erōs* in a good sense; thus Justin (*Dialogue* 8, 1) speaks of the fire kindled in his soul and the *erōs* for the prophets which came over him. But for Ignatius the word has a bad sense, as in *Corpus Hermeticum* 1, 18-19 and the Acts of John 68 (Schlier p. 152). Is this usage Gnostic? Certainly the Valentinians (Irenaeus, *Adv. haer.* 1, 2, 4) could speak of the Desire of Wisdom being separated and crucified by Limit (cf. R. M. Grant, *Gnosticism: An Anthology* [London–New York, 1961], 166), but their idea, like that of Ignatius, seems to be based on two Pauline verses: Galatians 5:24 ("those who belong to Christ Jesus have crucified the flesh with its passions and desires") and 6:14 ("the cross of our Lord Jesus Christ, through which the world has been crucified for me and I for the world"). The idea is not Gnostic as such. Indeed, in the second Gnostic Apocalypse of James it is *erōs* that is identified as the grace of the Father (A. Böhlig–P. Labib, *Koptisch-Gnostische Apokalypsen aus Codex V von Nag Hammadi* [Halle-Wittenberg, 1963], p. 85, line 8).

Preiss pp. 199-202 sharply contrasts Ignatius' desire to die with Paul's serenity expressed in Philippians 1. But (1) Ignatius was not Paul and he had actually been condemned to death, and (2) Paul

2. I beg you with this short letter: believe me. Jesus Christ will make plain to you that I speak the truth, and he is the mouth that cannot lie, by which the Father truly spoke. 3. Pray for me that I may attain. I am writing to you in accordance not with the flesh but with the purpose of God. If I suffer, you favored me; if I am rejected [cf. 1 Cor. 9:27], you hated me.

---

himself speaks of his desire to depart and be with Christ (Phil. 1:23). The difference has been exaggerated.

The fire which loves matter (i.e., *erōs;* cf. 1 Cor. 7:9) has been quenched and replaced by living water. This picture of water is not only Johannine (John. 4:10; 7:38) but also Eucharistic (and therefore magical-sacramental, Bartsch p. 110); Maurer p. 43 regards it as not certainly either Johannine or sacramental. If with Lightfoot and the interpolator of Ignatius' letters we were to read "water bubbling up in me," the text would be very close to John 4:14 and to quotations of John by Gnostics (Lightfoot p. 225), but there is no reason to make this change. The living water, like the Spirit (Philad. 7:1), can speak within Ignatius and direct him to the Father. Presumably the figure is a commonplace of Jewish Christianity; cf. J. Daniélou, *Primitive Christian Symbols* (Baltimore, 1964), 42-48.

The food of corruption is simply perishable food, or perhaps food incapable of producing real life, like the manna of John 6:49. Ignatius desires Eucharistic bread, the bread of God (John 6:33) which is the flesh of Jesus (John 6:51; Philad. 4:1; Smyrn. 7:1)—the human Jesus, descended from David (Eph. 18:2; 20:2; Trall. 9:1; Smyrn. 1:1)—and he also desires Jesus' Eucharistic blood to drink (John 6:53-56). This blood is not simply blood but imperishable love, as in Trallians 8:1 (cf. Smyrn. 1:1; joy, Philad. inscr.).

It should be noted that in this passage the Eucharist is not, or not only, a meal in which Christians presently participate (as in Eph. 13:1; Philad. 4:1; Smyrn. 7:1; 8:1) but a future event presumably associated, as in John 6:54, with the resurrection of believers (cf. Eph. 11:1-2).

8:1–3. Ignatius no longer desires (not "loves" here, against Bauer p. 252) to live in a merely human way—as described in chapter 7—and he can reach the goal of death and resurrection if the Romans agree. For the form of his next sentence see on Ephesians 2:2.

As Bauer p. 253 observes, Christian writers often speak of the brevity of their letters—even when, it should be added, they are not very brief. In their view the presence of brevity means the absence of sophistry (Justin, *Apology* 1, 14, 5). Jesus Christ will reveal the truth of what Ignatius says, presumably when the Romans bear in mind what he taught about becoming his disciple. And Jesus' own

E. Final Greetings (9:1–10:3)

9 In your prayer remember the church in Syria which has God for its shepherd instead of me. Only Jesus Christ will be its bishop—and your love. 2. I am ashamed to be called one of them, for I am not worthy, since I am the least of them and an "abortion" [1 Cor. 15:8-9]; but I have obtained mercy to be someone [cf. 1 Cor. 7:25], if I may attain to God. 3. My spirit salutes you, as does the love of the churches which have received me in the name of Jesus Christ [cf. Matt. 10:40-41], not as a transient visitor. For even those churches which do not lie on my road (humanly speaking) went before me from one city to another.

10 I write you this from Smyrna through the Ephesians, most worthy of blessing. With me, along with many others, is Crocus,

---

words are true because he is the "mouth" by which the Father spoke. The notion of Jesus as the mouth of the Father is expressed in two documents close to Jewish Christianity and Gnosticism, Ode of Solomon 12:11 and the Gospel of Truth (p. 26, 34).

Ignatius does not say what he wishes to attain, but it is obviously to martyrdom and God. The Romans will favor him by letting him suffer; they will really have hated him if he is rejected by God. Here *thelein* does mean "love" (so Bauer p. 253; Preiss p. 221 n. 40) or "favor," but this is not always its meaning.

9:1–3. As in other letters written before the arrival of news from Antioch (Eph. 21:1-2; Magn. 14:1; Trall. 13:1), Ignatius asks the Romans to "remember" the Syrian church. He has been its shepherd (cf. Acts 20:28; 1 Pet. 5:2-3; Philad. 2:1); now God acts directly without a human agent; Jesus Christ is bishop of Antioch (cf. 1 Pet. 2:25: "the Shepherd and Bishop of your souls"), along with the love of the Roman community, which also must watch over the Christians of Antioch.

Once more Ignatius imitates Paul's words in 1 Corinthians 15:8-9 and applies them to himself and his unworthiness; he has, however, "obtained mercy to be" (1 Cor. 7:25; cf. 1 Tim. 1:13) someone in the future (as he is not now, Eph. 3:1), if he attains to God.

His spirit (cf. Eph. 18:1; Trall. 13:3; Smyrn. 10:2) greets them, for he is not yet present with them (cf. 1 Cor. 5:3; Col. 2:5); so does the love of the Asian churches (Trall. 13:1; Philad. 11:2; Smyrn. 12:1) which have wonderfully received him even when they did not lie on his direct route (he means the Ephesians, the Magnesians, and the Trallians, but not the Philadelphians).

10:1–3. In Ignatius' mind the Ephesians are especially "worthy

a name dear to me. 2. Concerning those who have preceded me
from Syria to Rome for the glory of God, I believe that you have
information. Tell them that I am near, for all of them are worthy
of God and of you, and it is fitting for you to refresh them in
every way. 3. I am writing you this on the ninth before the
kalends of September [August 24]. Farewell to the end, in the
endurance of Jesus Christ [cf. 2 Thess. 3:5].

---

of blessing" (Eph. inscr.; cf. 12:2); they have sent Crocus to assist
him (Eph. 2:1); perhaps Crocus is bearing the letter to Rome.

Other Syrian martyrs have preceded him; perhaps they include
Zosimus and Rufus, mentioned with Ignatius by Polycarp (Phil.
9:1); in any event, the Romans presumably know who they are,
and should "refresh" them.

This is the only date in Ignatius' letters; unfortunately it does
not include the year. His farewell is based on something like 2
Thessalonians 3:5, "the endurance of Christ," and Matthew 10:22;
24:13, "he who endures to the end will be saved" (cf. Eph. 14:2).

PHILADELPHIANS

OUTLINE

Salutation
A. The Philadelphian bishop (1:1-2)
B. Exhortation to unity (2:1–4:1)
C. The problem at Philadelphia (5:1–6:2)
D. Ignatius at Philadelphia (6:3–8:2)
E. The Old Testament and the gospel (9:1-2)
F. The church of Philadelphia and the church of Antioch (10:1-2)
G. Personal notes and final greetings (11:1-2)

Philadelphians

Ignatius, also called Theophorus, to the church of God the Father and the Lord Jesus Christ which is at Philadelphia in Asia, granted mercy and established in the harmony of God and rejoicing in the passion of our Lord without doubting and fully assured of all mercy by his resurrection: I salute her in the blood of Jesus Christ, which is eternal and lasting joy, especially if Christians are at one with the bishop and the presbyters and deacons who with him have been appointed by the intention of Jesus Christ, who established them, in accordance with his own will, in security by his Holy Spirit.

A. The Philadelphian bishop (1:1-2)

1 I know that your bishop obtained his ministry, related to the whole community, "not from himself or through men" [cf. Gal

---

Salutation. Ignatius' salutation is divided into two parts: (1) a description of the ideal condition of the Philadelphian church, given mercy and established (Eph. 12:1; "mercy" in Rom. inscr.; Smyrn. inscr.) in God's harmony (Magn. 6:1; 15:1), rejoicing in the passion "without doubting" (Rom. inscr.), "fully assured" (Magn. 11:1; Smyrn. 1:1) by the resurrection; and (2) a greeting (a) in the blood of Jesus Christ, which is eternal joy ("love" in Trall. 8:1; Rom. 7:3; cf. Smyrn. 1:1)—especially (b) if there is unity with the bishop and the other ministers appointed in accordance with the purpose of Jesus Christ (Eph. 3:2) and established by his Holy Spirit (the Spirit is Jesus Christ, Magn. 15:1; it was at work in Ignatius at Philadelphia, 7:1-2). For the Spirit as the Spirit of Jesus cf. Paul, Romans 8:9-11; Acts 16:6-7. Jesus' blood is identified with the Holy Spirit in the Gospel of Philip (p. 105, 6-7); cf. R. McL. Wilson, *The Gospel of Philip* (London, 1962), 89.

1:1-2. The Philadelphian bishop, whose name Ignatius does not mention, has a ministry or office essentially analogous to that of the apostle Paul, whose words Ignatius paraphrases in describing it.

1:1] or for vainglory, but in the love of God the Father and the Lord Jesus Christ. I was impressed by his gentleness because when silent he can do more than those who speak in vain. 2. For he is attuned to the commandments as a harp is to its strings. Therefore my soul blesses his godly mind, recognizing it as virtuous and perfect, and his immovability and freedom from wrath, with all the gentleness characteristic of the living God.

B. Exhortation to unity (2:1–4:1)

2 As children of the light [cf. Paul, Eph. 5:8] of truth, flee from division and wrong teaching; where the shepherd is, follow there as sheep [cf. John 10:10-12, etc.]. 2. For there are many specious wolves who by evil pleasure take captive those who are running for God; but they will have no place in your unity.

Since this bishop is devoted to the unity of the church, he did not assume office with a view to empty deceit (again Pauline, Phil. 2:3). His godlike and, Christian (Eph. 10:3) gentleness may have been rather excessive, to judge from chapters 6–8, but Ignatius prefers to suggest that his silence was truly creative (cf. Eph. 15:2; the meekness of the Trallian bishop, Trall. 3:2-3).

The commandments with which the bishop is in tune (cf. Eph. 4:1-2) presumably consist primarily of the commandment of love (John 13:34; 14:15; 15:10), and Ignatius' "soul" (only here; cf. 11:2) blesses him for his immovable (Smyrn. 1:1; Polyc. 1:1) quality —his freedom from the wrath (only here) which might have characterized his dealings with his congregation. It is possible that Ignatius mentions "the living God" to remind the Philadelphians that behind the bishop lies the wrath of God himself (cf. 1 Thess. 1:9-10; Heb. 10:31).

More probably, he views the life of God as full of virtue and perfection—involving immutability and freedom from wrath. For similar divine attributes compare Polycarp 3:2 commentary. Ignatius lays little emphasis on God's wrath (but cf. Eph. 11:1); though like his successor Theophilus (*Ad Autol.*, 1, 3) he evidently believes in it, he does not regard it as primarily characteristic of God.

2:1–4:1. Christians are "children of the light of truth" (Ignatius himself wants to receive "pure light," Rom. 6:2; this tension between present and future is typical of early Christianity); compare the Pauline expression "children of light" (Eph. 5:8) and the Johannine "true light" (John 1:9; 1 John 2:8). As in the Pauline text, identification is followed by exhortation—here to follow where the shepherd is (John 10:1-16; Acts 20:28-30; 1 Pet. 5:2-4). With the

3 Abstain from the evil weeds which Jesus Christ does not cultivate because they are not the planting of the Father—not that I
found division among you; what I found was filtering-out. 2. For
as many as belong to God and Jesus Christ, these are with the
bishop. And as many as repent and come to the unity of the
church, these also will belong to God so that they may be living
in accordance with Jesus Christ. 3. "Do not be deceived, my
brothers": if anyone follows a maker of schism he "will not
inherit the kingdom of God" [1 Cor. 6:9-10]; if anyone walks in
strange doctrine he has no share in the passion.

4 Be eager, therefore, to use one Eucharist—for there is one
flesh of our Lord Jesus Christ and one cup for union with his
blood, one sanctuary, as there is one bishop, together with the
presbytery and the deacons my fellow slaves—so that, whatever
you do, you do it in relation to God [cf. 1 Cor. 10:31; Col. 3:17].

---

mention of "wolves" (John; Acts) Ignatius combines the devil's
leading men captive from the life set before them (Eph. 17:1) and
then turns to the race set before them (cf. Heb. 12:1-2) and speaks
of them as God-runners. The wolves will find no place if Christians
remain in the unity of which he is going to speak.

3:1–3. The wolves can also be called "evil weeds" (cf. Eph.
10:3; Trall. 6:1; 11:1; also Matt. 7:15-16); Jesus Christ does not
cultivate them because they are tares planted by the devil (Matt.
13:38-39; for the Father, cultivator of the vine which is Jesus, cf.
John 15:1), not by the Father (cf. Trall. 11:1; Matt. 15:13). Among
the Philadelphians there is no real division but simply a process of
filtering out the good from the bad (cf. Rom. inscr.).

As the filtering goes on, those who belong to God and Jesus are
with the bishop; others repent and come to unity (8:1; Smyrn.
4:1; 5:3); still others "will not inherit the kingdom of God" (1
Cor. 6:9-10; Eph. 16:1) and are not in union with the passion—
hence not with the resurrection (Magn. 5:2; Philad. inscr.; Smyrn.
5:3).

For the Jewish Christian idea of the Church as God's "plantation"
see J. Daniélou, *Primitive Christian Symbols* (Baltimore, 1964),
24-35.

4:1. If the Philadelphians are to avoid schism, they must be
zealous to preserve unity (Paul's terms in Eph. 4:3); Ignatius continues to imitate Pauline expressions while modifying them. Where
Paul had spoken of "one body, and one Spirit . . . one hope of your
calling; one Lord, one faith, one baptism, one God and Father of
all" (Eph. 4:4-6), Ignatius' language is more explicitly sacramental

C. The problem at Philadelphia (5:1–6:2)

5 My brothers, I overflow with love for you, and I am exceedingly joyful to be watching out for your safety—not I, but Jesus Christ [1 Cor. 15:10; cf. Gal. 2:20], for whom I am in bonds, though I fear all the more because I am still imperfect. But your prayer to God will make me perfect so that I may attain to the lot in which I was given mercy, fleeing to the gospel as to the flesh of Jesus and to the apostles as to the presbytery of the church. 2. The prophets we also love because they made a proclamation related to the gospel and set their hope on him and were waiting for him; by believing in him they were saved, being united with Jesus Christ. Worthy of love and admiration, they are saints, attested by Jesus Christ and numbered together with us in the gospel of the common hope [cf. 1 Tim. 1:1].

(as in 1 Cor. 10:16-17). There is to be one Eucharist, because there is one flesh of Jesus (cf. Smyrn. 7:1) and one cup for union with his blood ("cup" only here in Ignatius; cf. 1 Cor. 10:16) and one sanctuary (*thysiastērion* in Ignatius means "altar" only in Rom. 2:2) and one bishop along with the other ministers. If there is only one Eucharist, the Philadelphians will be acting "in accordance with God" (cf. 1 Cor. 10:31; Col. 3:17). Ignatius goes very little beyond Paul's expressions in 1 Corinthians 10:16-17; like John, he prefers the word "flesh" to "body" (both are translations of the Hebrew *basar*; cf. J. Bonsirven, "Hoc est corpus meum," *Biblica* 29 [1948], 205-219). On deacons as fellow slaves see on Ephesians 2:1.

5:1-2. Ignatius loves the Philadelphians, in spite of everything, and either is "consumed by love" for them (so Bauer) or is being poured out as a sacrifice for them (cf. Mark 14:24 and parallels; 1 Clem. 7:4; Ignatius, Rom. 2:2). He rejoices to watch over them (cf. Isa. 41:10)—not he himself but Jesus Christ (a Pauline expression, 1 Cor. 15:10; Gal. 2:20; cf. Trall. 6:1) for whom he is in bonds (cf. "in Jesus Christ," Trall. 1:1; Rom. 1:1). He fears as well as rejoices, for he is still imperfect (Trall. 6:1; Paul, Phil. 3:12); but the Philadelphians' prayer will perfect him (Eph. 1:1; 3:1; Polyc. 7:3); he will be made perfect with God (Eph. 19:3) and will "attain" to the lot (Eph. 11:2; Trall. 12:3; Rom. 1:2; Paul, Col. 1:12) in which God has already had mercy on him (Rom. 9:2; cf. 1 Cor. 7:25; 1 Tim. 1:13)—as he takes refuge in the gospel of Jesus' flesh (cf. faith as the Lord's flesh, Trall. 8:1) and the apostles as the church's presbytery (vice versa, Magn. 6:1; Trall. 2:2; 3:1; Smyrn. 8:1).

Christians also love the prophets—thus we seem to have some-

6 But if anyone interprets Judaism to you, do not listen to him. For it is better to hear Christianity from a man who has received circumcision than Judaism from one who has not. Both of them, if they do not speak of Jesus Christ, are tombstones to me and graves of the dead [cf. Matt. 23:27] on which nothing but human names are inscribed. 2. Flee, then, from the evil arts and snares of the prince of this age, lest you be afflicted by his scheming and grow weak in love. Come together, all of you, with an undivided heart.

---

thing like, or leading toward, a collection of authorities related to writings: gospel, apostles, prophets—for they too foreshadowed the gospel, set their hope on Jesus (cf. 11:2), and waited for him (Magn. 9:2). They were saved by faith in him and were united with him (his disciples, Magn. 9:2)—loveworthy and admiration-worthy saints (i.e., Christians, Magn. 3:1; Trall. inscr.; Smyrn. 1:2) attested (Eph. 12:2) by Jesus Christ (cf. 7:2) and numbered (cf. W. C. van Unnik in *Revue d'histoire et de philosophie religieuses* 42 [1962], 237-246) with the rest of the elect in the gospel which sets forth, and is, the common hope (Eph. 1:2; Jesus Christ, Eph. 21:2; Philad. 11:2).

6:1–2. Advocacy of "Judaism" (i.e., Judaistic Christianity) is to be discouraged on the ground that it is better to hear about "Christianity" (a word first found in Magn. 10:3) from Jewish Christians than about Judaism from a Gentile. Ignatius seems to have Gentile converts to Jewish Christianity in mind, not unlike those whom Paul describes as not keeping the law but advocating circumcision (Gal. 6:13) or the Philadelphians of Revelation 3:9, who "call themselves, but are not, Jews." He compares his opponents with "tombstones and sepulchres of dead men," just as in Matthew 23:27 hypocritical scribes and Pharisees are compared with "whited sepulchres"—though the emphasis in his comparison shifts from whitewashing to the inscription of nothing but human names on the stones. This may imply that Christian tombstones already bore a cross or the name of Jesus.

Heterodox teaching is equivalent to the intrigues of "the prince of this age" (see on Eph. 17:1), as in Revelation 2:9 pseudo Jews belong to "the synagogue of Satan." To be afflicted by his scheming means to grow weak in love, that is, to lose the unity of the community and its expression in works; the remedy for such a condition is to meet for worship with an undivided heart (cf. Trall. 13:2). God, unity, and love stand on one side; the devil, division, and heterodoxy on the other. Because of his experiences at Philadelphia, Ignatius uses "division(s)" five times in this letter, only once elsewhere (Smyrn. 7:2).

D. Ignatius at Philadelphia (6:3–8:2)

3. I give thanks to my God [Phil. 1:3] that I have a good conscience in relation to you, and that no one can boast secretly or openly that I was a burden to any [cf. 2 Cor. 11:9; 12:16; 1 Thess. 2:6, 9] in matters either small or great. And I pray for all among whom I spoke, so that they may not keep (the blame) as a testimony against themselves.

7 For even if some desired to deceive me in a merely human way, the Spirit is not deceived, for it is from God. For it "knows

---

6:3. "I thank my God," Ignatius writes—imitating an expression fairly common in the Pauline epistles (Rom. 1:8; 1 Cor. 1:4; Phil. 1:3; Philem. 4; cf. 1 Cor. 14:18)—"that I have a clear conscience in relation to you." He means that he lacks any consciousness of wrongdoing (cf. 1 Cor. 4:4, a verse he reflects in Rom. 5:1). The wrongdoing must be related to his burdening anyone, and again his language and his ideas are Pauline; Paul says that by working he laid burdens on none of his converts (1 Thess. 2:9; 2 Cor. 11:9; 12:16). Ignatius means that the Philadelphians did not "refresh" him (see on Eph. 2:1); had they done so, they might have claimed that he burdened them. His irony is not unlike Paul's. Bauer p. 259 seems to misunderstand when he says that Ignatius' opponents criticized him for burdening them with his views. Such an interpretation is possible in the light of chapters 7–8, but in view of the Pauline precedent it is probably not justified. Ignatius seems to be following a synoptic thought pattern when he speaks of their failure to assist him as becoming a testimony against them; the earliest missionaries were to shake off dust for a testimony against those who would not receive or hear them (Mark 6:11; cf. Luke 9:5; Matt. 10:14). In the same context in Matthew (10:19-20) we hear of the Spirit's speaking through martyrs, and Ignatius refers to the Spirit's speaking through himself in his next chapter.

Some Philadelphians undoubtedly objected to Ignatius' ideas about the gospel and the Church, but their ideas were expressed in their unwillingness to provide gifts for his support and encouragement. Later they treated Ignatius' followers in the same fashion, though others at Philadelphia (those with the bishop, presumably) behaved better (11:1; note the repetition of "testify" and "I thank God on your behalf").

7:1–2.   Though some desired to mislead (the word is so used only here and in Magn. 3:2) Ignatius, they could not do so, for he was inspired by the Spirit (of truth, John 14:17). This Spirit, like Jesus (John 8:14; cf. John 3:8), "knows whence it comes and whither it goes," and tests the secrets of men's minds (cf. 1 Cor. 2:10; 14:24-25). Ignatius recalls an occasion at Philadelphia when he was

whence it comes and whither it goes" [John 8:14; 3:8] and exposes secrets [1 Cor. 2:10; 14:24-25]. When I was with you I cried out, I spoke with a loud voice, God's own voice: "Pay attention to the bishop and the presbytery and deacons." 2. Some suspected me of saying this because I had advance information about the division of some persons; but he for whom I am in bonds is my witness that I did not know it from any human being. The Spirit made proclamation, saying this: "Do nothing apart from the bishop; keep your flesh as the temple of God [2 Clem. 9:3]; love unity; flee from divisions; be imitators of Jesus Christ as he is of his Father."

8 I did what I could as a man devoted to unity. But God does not dwell where there is division and wrath. The Lord forgives all who repent, if they repent and turn toward the unity of God and the council of the bishop. I am confident that by the grace of Jesus Christ he will loose every bond from you. 2. But I exhort

---

obviously prophesying in the Spirit: he spoke with a loud cry, the voice of God (on this term see A.-G. 879), and counseled devotion to the bishop, the presbytery, and the deacons.

Some Philadelphians suspected that Ignatius had received advance information about the division in their community (his letters, which they did not possess, show that it was unnecessary). He replies that the one (Jesus Christ, cf. Trall. 1:1; Rom. 1:1) in or for whom he is a prisoner (cf. Col. 4:3) is his witness (cf. Paul, Rom. 1:9; Phil. 1:8; 1 Thess. 2:5); his knowledge of the situation came from no "human flesh" (cf. "flesh and blood," Matt. 16:17) but from the Spirit. What the Spirit said was based on early Christian tradition. "Do nothing apart from the bishop" (cf. Magn. 4:1; 7:1; Trall. 2:2; 7:2; Smyrn. 8:1-2; the bishop does nothing apart from God, Polyc. 4:1); "keep your flesh as the temple of God" (2 Clem. 9:3; cf. 1 Cor. 3:16-17; 6:19; 2 Cor. 6:16); "love unity" (cf. Magn. 13:2; Trall. 11:2); "flee from divisions" (Philad. 2:1; Smyrn. 7:2). Finally, imitate Jesus Christ (cf. 1 Cor. 11:1) as he imitates his Father (a theme from John 5:19). Ignatius also speaks of imitating the Lord (Eph. 10:3; cf. 1 Thess. 1:6), of imitating God (Eph. 1:1; Trall. 1:2; cf. Paul's Eph. 5:1, but Ignatius means imitating Jesus Christ, cf. Rom. 6:3), and even of imitating the Ephesian deacon Burrhus (see on Smyrn. 12:1).

8:1–2. At Philadelphia, Ignatius did what was suitable for a man "made for" unity (similar expressions in Eph. 2:2; Smyrn. 1:1). Where there is division (the word five times in this letter, once in Smyrnaeans), God does not dwell—since God dwells in the temple

you to do nothing with partisan spirit—instead, in accordance with what you have learned of Christ. I heard some say, "Unless I find it in the 'charters,' I do not believe it in the gospel." And when I told them, "It is written," they answered me, "That is the question." But for me the "charters" are Jesus Christ; the inviolable charters are his cross and death and his resurrection and the faith which exists through him. In these, through your prayer, I desire to be justified.

E. The Old Testament and the gospel (9:1-2)

9 The priests are noble, but the High Priest, entrusted with the

---

of the united believers who flee from divisions (7:2). But God forgives those who repent and come to the unity of the Church (3:2), that is, to the unity characteristic of God and to the council of the bishop (comparable to the council of the apostles, Magn. 6:1; or of God, Trall. 3:1). This repentance and forgiveness are consequent upon the grace of Jesus Christ (an expression frequent in Paul's letters; cf. also 11:1; Magn. 8:2; Smyrn. 6:2), who will loose every bond (of wickedness, Eph. 19:3; cf. Isa. 58:6) from believers.

Ignatius explicitly exhorts them to do nothing with, or in, selfish ambition but to act in accordance with Christian discipleship; the contrast recalls Paul's words in Philippians 2:3 (cf. 1:17); 2:5-11. The contrast also recalls a specific event at Philadelphia. There were those who said (from selfish ambition) that they would not believe in the gospel (the same expression as in Mark 1:15) unless they found it (presumably predicted or prefigured) in the "original documents" (presumably the Old Testament) themselves. These critics were presumably Judaizers; Ignatius replied by stating, "It is written" (the usual formula for Old Testament quotations; cf. Eph. 5:3; Magn. 12:1), and they answered, "That is the question." In other words, they did not accept his Old Testament exegesis, probably the kind indicated in Magnesians 8:2–9:2 and about to be set forth here in chapter 9. Ignatius now passes from reminiscence to kerygmatic statement (cf. Gal. 2:14-21), proclaiming that for him the sacred documents ("original" in the sense of Magn. 10:3) consist of Jesus Christ with his cross, death, and resurrection (cf. 1 Cor. 1:22-24), and the faith which came into existence through him (Acts 3:16; cf. Heb. 12:2). Ignatius desires to be "justified" by the saving events and by faith (a Pauline idea), along with the community's common prayer (cf. 5:1; on prayer, see on Eph. 5:2). For this combination see Paul, Philippians 1:19. The idea of "justification" occurs in Ignatius only here and in Romans 5:1 (a Pauline allusion).

9:1–2. The Old Testament priests are good, that is, they have a

Holy of Holies, is nobler; he alone has been entrusted with the secrets of God; he himself is the door to the Father [John 10:7, 9; 14:6], through which enter Abraham and Isaac and Jacob, and the prophets and the apostles and the Church. All these are in the unity of God [cf. Ps. 117:20 LXX]. 2. But the gospel has something distinctive: the coming of the Savior, our Lord Jesus Christ, his passion and resurrection. For the beloved prophets made a proclamation related to him; but the gospel is the perfection of imperishability. All things together are good, if you believe with love.

F. The church of Philadelphia and the church of Antioch (10:1-2)

10 Since it has been reported to me that, in accordance with your prayer and the compassion which you have in Christ Jesus [cf. Phil. 1:8], the church at Antioch in Syria is at peace, it is fitting for you as a church of God to appoint a deacon to carry

---

part to play in the plan of salvation; but the High Priest (Jesus, as in Hebrews and 1 Clem. 36:1, etc.) is greater, since he has been entrusted with the Holy of Holies (Heb. 9:3) and God's secrets. Because he is "the door to the Father" (John 10:7, 9; 14:6; Maurer pp. 30-34), he is the one through whom the patriarchs, the prophets, the apostles, and indeed the Church, enter and are united in God's unity.

Priests and High Priest in the Old Testament, however, are inferior to the gospel, since it proclaims the coming (*parousia*, only here in Ignatius; past, as probably in 2 Pet. 1:16, though in the New Testament usually future), suffering, and resurrection of "the Savior" (Eph. 1:1; Magn. inscr.; Smyrn. 7:1) Jesus Christ. The "beloved" ("divine" in Magn. 8:2) prophets foreshadowed him (or the gospel, 5:2), but the gospel is the consummation of imperishability, since Jesus breathed imperishability upon the Church (Eph. 17:1); the goal of Christians is imperishability and eternal life (Polyc. 2:3). Compare 2 Clement 7:5; 14:5; 20:5; also 1 Corinthians 15:50-54. All together—Old Testament and gospel—are good (related to salvation) if Christians combine faith with love, as in Ephesians 1:1 (see commentary).

10:1-2. Ignatius has learned, after reaching Troas from Smyrna, that the situation of the church at Antioch (now explicitly so located; not earlier) has improved; this is what the messengers came to tell him (11:1). The church is now at peace. We do not know what the causes of its unpeaceful state had been, although the temporary lack of a human bishop was undoubtedly one of them

out God's mission there, to congratulate those who are assembled
and to glorify his Name. 2. Blessed in Jesus Christ is he who will
be judged worthy of such a ministry, and you too will be glorified.
If you have the will to do so, it is not impossible for you to do
this for God's Name—just as the neighboring churches have sent
bishops, and others presbyters and deacons.

G. Personal notes and final greetings (11:1-2)

11 As for Philo, the deacon from Cilicia, a man of good report,
who is now serving me in the word of God with Rheus Agath-
opos, an elect man who has followed me from Syria and has
renounced human life—these bear witness for you, and I also give
thanks to God for you [1 Cor. 1:4], that you received them as
the Lord received you. May those who dishonored them be re-

(Rom. 9:1). Presumably the arrest and deportation of Ignatius,
and of others before him (Rom. 10:2), upset the church; the crisis
probably intensified divisions, for Judaizers could claim to be Jews
(cf. Rev. 2:9; 3:9) and Docetists could easily deny (the human)
Jesus, as Ignatius implies they should (Trall. 10:1) and as Gnostics
actually did. The peace was related to the restoration of church
order (Smyrn. 11:2). Therefore Ignatius asks the Philadelphians
to send a deacon as a delegate to congratulate them because of what
has taken place. Churches nearer Antioch, he knows, have sent
bishops, while others have sent presbyters and deacons. In view of
the situation in Philadelphia, it is unlikely that the bishop could
be spared, just as Polycarp is to send someone, not to go himself
(Polyc. 8:2).

It is tempting to infer that the delegates were assembling for the
consecration of Ignatius' successor but, which nothing he says ex-
cludes the possibility, there is no mention of such an event. Presbyters
as well as bishops, at the end of the second century, took part in
episcopal consecrations, as we learn from the *Apostolic Tradition*
of Hippolytus (presbyters earlier, perhaps in 1 Tim. 4:14). Ignatius
insists that the offices of ministers are derived from Jesus Christ
(Eph. 3:2; Philad. inscr.; 1:1) but says nothing of apostolic suces-
sion as such.

11:1-2. At Troas, Ignatius has been joined by the Cilician
deacon Philo and by another deacon, Rheus Agathopus, from Syria
(cf. Smyrn. 10:1). The latter's renunciation of "this life" probably
implies that he is continuing to Rome with Ignatius, though it may
simply mean that he is devoting himself to the Church. Both men
have come from Cilicia to Philadelphia to Smyrna and finally to
Troas. The Philadelphians generally received them as Christian

deemed by the grace of Jesus Christ. 2. The love of the brothers at Troas salutes you. I write you from there through Burrhus, who was sent with me by the Ephesians and Smyrnaeans as a token of respect. The Lord Jesus Christ will reward them—on whom they set their hope in flesh and soul and spirit, faith and love and harmony. Farewell in Christ Jesus, our common hope [cf. 1 Tim. 1:1].

---

brothers, but some, probably the heterodox (see on 6:3) "dishonored" them, presumably dissociating themselves from Ignatius and perhaps from martyrdom.

The Christians at Troas—where there had been a church since Paul's time (Acts 20:5-12)—sent their greetings to Philadelphia, whence Ignatius is "writing to you through Burrhus." Lake (p. 251) translates *dia* not as "through" but as "by the hand of," evidently relying on the parallel provided by 1 Peter 5:12: "I have written you a brief letter *dia* Silvanus"—and Silvanus is probably the scribe of the letter, although in Acts 15:27 Silas, probably the same person, is the bearer of documents from the apostolic council. The word *dia* is ambiguous. It has been conjectured that when Ignatius mentions Burrhus to the Ephesians and asks for his continued services (Eph. 2:1), he has in mind his acting as scribe for the letters, for example, those to "all the churches" (Rom. 4:1). This conjecture is not altogether certain, however, for the letters explicitly described as *"dia* Burrhus" (Philadelphians, Smyrnaeans) may have been carried by rather than dictated to Burrhus. Perhaps a more convincing parallel is provided by Polycarp's letter to the Philippians (14:1); he writes to them *"per Crescentum"* and commends him to the letter's recipients (as Paul does; cf. O. Roller, *Das Formular der paulinischen Briefe* [Stuttgart, 1933], 132). We should conclude that Burrhus, as Ephesian deacon, had his expenses paid by the churches of Ephesus and Smyrna so that he could carry Ignatius' letters to Smyrna and Philadelphia. We cannot tell whether or not Ignatius dictated letters to him, though he may have done so.

Ignatius expresses a benediction not upon the Philadelphians but upon the Ephesians and the Smyrnaeans, who have set their hope on Jesus in "flesh and soul and spirit" (a triad reminiscent of 1 Thess. 5:23) and in "faith and love and harmony" (another triad reminiscent of 1 Cor. 13:13); Ignatius substitutes "harmony" for "hope" because he has already mentioned the latter and wants to emphasize the former. On the formulations see on Magnesians 13:1; on "our hope," see on Ephesians 21:2.

SMYRNAEANS

OUTLINE

Salutation
A. The common Christian faith (1:1-2)
B. Warning against Docetic doctrine (2:1–6:1)
C. Warning against Docetic practice (6:2–9:1)
D. Ignatius' thanksgiving (9:2–10:2)
E. The church of Smyrna and the church of Antioch (11:1-3)
F. Final greetings (12:1–13:2)

Smyrnaeans

Salutation

Ignatius, also called Theophorus, to the church of God the Father
and the beloved Jesus Christ which has mercifully been given
every gift [cf. 1 Cor. 1:7], filled with faith and love, not lacking in
any gift, most worthy of God and bearing holy things; at Smyrna
in Asia; abundant greeting in a blameless spirit and the word
of God.

A. The common Christian faith (1:1-2)

1 I give glory to Jesus Christ, the God who made you so wise;
for I know that you are established in immovable faith, as if you
were nailed in flesh and spirit to the cross of the Lord Jesus

---

Salutation. The structure of this salutation is quite simple, perhaps because Ignatius knows the Smyrnaeans' representatives so well.
The church (1) enjoys every gift of grace (1 Cor. 1:7), (2) has been
filled (cf. Rom. inscr.) with faith and love, (3) lacks no gift of grace
(1 Cor. 1:7 again), (4) is most worthy of God (cf. 11:1; Magn. 1:2;
Polyc. 7:2) and bears holy things (Eph. 9:2). As in all the letters except Philadelphians, Ignatius sends "abundant greeting," here in a
"blameless spirit" (cf. Eph. inscr.) and in the word of God (cf. 10:1;
Philad. 11:1)—the Christian message or gospel. For a discussion of the
ministry in Smyrnaeans see M. H. Shepherd, Jr., "Smyrna in the Ignatian Letters: A Study in Church Order," *Journal of Religion* 20
(1940), 141-159.

1:1–2. Ignatius gives glory to Jesus Christ (cf. Eph. 2:2) and,
partly because of his theology (Christ is God), partly because he
elsewhere relates "glory" to God (Eph. 13:1; Magn. 15:1; Rom. 10:2;
Polyc. 4:3; 7:2), speaks of him as the God who has made the Smyrnaeans "wise" (a reminiscence of 1 Cor. 1:18 ff.; Bauer p. 264)—by his
gifts of grace, as indicated in the preface to the letter. Ignatius knows
from personal encounter that their faith is immutable; they are
practically "nailed" to the cross as Jesus himself actually was (1:2),
and their love is analogous to their faith. They have "full conviction"

113

Christ and confirmed in love by the blood of Christ—being convinced [cf. Luke 1:1] concerning our Lord that he is

truly of the family of David as to the flesh,

Son of God by God's will and power [cf. Rom. 1:3-4],

truly born of a virgin,

baptized by John so that "all righteousness" might be "fulfilled" by him [Matt. 3:15],

2. truly nailed [John 20:25] for us in the flesh

under Pontius Pilate and the tetrarch Herod

(from the tree's fruit are we,

from his passion blessed by God),

so that he might set up an ensign [Isa. 5:26; 11:12, etc.] forever through the resurrection

for his saints and faithful

(whether among Jews or among Gentiles)

in the one body of his Church [Paul, Eph. 2:16].

(cf. Luke 1:1; the same term, in a similar context, in Magn. 11:1 and Philad. inscr.) in relation to "our Lord"; and Ignatius goes on to list the particulars of Christian faith. (1) He was humanly descended from David but Son of God in accordance with God's will and power—here Ignatius imitates Romans 1:3-4; (2) he was truly or really born of a virgin (cf. Eph. 7:2; 18:2; 19:1; Trall. 9:1); (3) he was baptized by John so that all righteousness might be fulfilled (clearly a reference, at first- or second-hand, to Matt. 3:15, as in the Gospel of Philip, p. 120, 30-121, 1; contrast Eph. 18:2, imaginative rather than traditional); (4) under Pontius Pilate and Herod the tetrarch (the tradition of Luke-Acts; cf. also Justin, *Apology* 1, 40, 6; *Dialogue* 103, 4; Bauer p. 265), he was "nailed" (cf. John. 20:25)—to the "tree" (Ignatius impetuously neglects to say so)—and Christians derive their existence from this tree, which grew for them (cf. Trall. 11:2). (5) The tree is also a "standard" (Isa. 5:26; 11:12, etc.) raised forever through the resurrection, to gather God's "saints and faithful" (Col. 1:2; Eph. 1:1), both Jews and Gentiles, into the one body (Eph. 2:16) of his Church (Col. 1:18).

It is sometimes supposed that here, as in Ephesians 18:2 and Trallians 9:1-2, Ignatius is quoting from an early credal formulation. It is less venturesome to suppose, with J. N. D. Kelly (*Early Christian Creeds* [London, 1950], 68-69), that we have a "primitive Christological kerygma"—much of its details derived from Ignatius' familiarity with synoptic and Johannine formulations and with the Pauline epistles.

On the "tree" see on Trallians 11:2 and the Gospel of Truth (p. 18, 24-25): "He was nailed to the tree and became a fruit of the

B. Warning against Docetic doctrine (2:1–6:1)

2 For he suffered all this for us so that we might be saved; and he truly suffered just as he truly raised himself [cf. John 10:18]—not, as some unbelievers say, that he appeared to suffer—they are the apparent ones, and just as they think, so it will happen to them when they are incorporeal and demonic.

3 For I know and am confident that even after the resurrection he was in the flesh. 2. And when he came to those with Peter he said to them, "Take, handle me, and see that I am not an incorporeal demon" [cf. Luke 24:39]. And they immediately touched him and believed, being mingled with his flesh and spirit. There-

---

knowledge of the Father." But note that the vaguely "Gnostic" note—"knowledge"—in the Gospel of Truth is lacking in both passages in Ignatius.

2:1. The suffering already described (1:2) took place for our salvation. Unless the suffering (and his raising of himself, as in John 10:18) was real, the salvation is obviously unreal; compare the somewhat similar line of argument in 1 Corinthians 15:12-17. As in Trallians 10:1, Ignatius claims that those who deny this reality merely seem to exist; what he means is that they lack the "true life" which is given only by faith in Christ Jesus (Trall. 9:2). Such men will actually perish after death (7:1), going to the unquenchable fire (Eph. 16:2) which will destroy their bodies and make them phantasmal (the words "bodiless" and "demonic" or "phantasmal" are based, as Bauer p. 266 points out, on the tradition quoted in 3:2).

3:1–3. Ignatius "knows and believes" (an emphatic combination, not used elsewhere, though the words are close together in Polyc. 7:3; cf. Paul, Rom. 14:14) that Jesus Christ was "in the flesh" not only before the resurrection (as in ch. 2) but also afterward.

He knows this as he knows facts about his correspondents (cf. Magn. 12:1; 14:1; Smyrn. 4:1; Polyc. 7:3). When the risen Lord came to Peter and his companions, he spoke to them with words close to, but different from, those set forth in Luke 24:39: "Handle me and see, that a spirit does not have flesh and bones such as you see I have." The meaning is the same, but the words, except for "handle me" and "see," are different. If Ignatius is quoting from Luke, he is quoting exceedingly freely; it is just as likely, if not more so, that he is relying on oral tradition (Koester pp. 45-56). Various ancient Christian writers tried to identify Ignatius' source: Origen (*Princ.* 1, praef. 8) says that it came from the Teaching of Peter; Eusebius (*H.E.* 3, 36, 11) does not know where it came from; Jerome (*De viris inlustribus* 2)

fore they despised death and were found to be above death. 3. And after the resurrection he ate and drank with them as a being of flesh [cf. Acts. 10:41; Luke 24:43], though he was spiritually united with the Father.

4 Now I warn you of these things, beloved, though I know that you agree with me. But I am guarding you in advance against beasts in human form, whom you must not only not receive but, if possible, not even meet—but only pray for them, if somehow they may repent. This is difficult, but Jesus Christ, our true life, has power over it. 2. For if these things were done by our Lord only in appearance, I too am in bonds in appearance. Why have I given myself up to death, to fire, to sword, to beasts? But near the sword is near God, with the beasts is with God. Only in the

---

says it is from the Gospel According to the Hebrews. There may be an allusion to Ignatius' words (or his source's) in Clement, *Exc. ex Theod.* 14, 1; but this does not help identify the saying. The statement that they touched him and believed recalls the story of "doubting Thomas" in John 20:24-29 but is not derived from it. For union in flesh and spirit see Magnesians 1:2; Romans inscription. If Ignatius was going to say that they were "mingled" with Jesus' flesh and spirit, he could not quote Luke's words about "spirit." Like Jesus himself (Heb. 12:2), they despised death and transcended it.

As in Acts 10:41 (cf. Luke 24:43), Jesus ate with his disciples, even though he was spiritually "united with the Father" (cf. John 10:30; 17:11, 22; Magn. 7:2).

4:1–2. The form of Ignatius' "warning" (the word only here and in Magn. 6:1) follows the pattern he uses elsewhere. He calls his readers "beloved" (Magn. 11:1; Trall. 8:1), suggests that they do not really need this counsel (Trall. 8:1; see on Eph. 4:1), and proceeds to "guard them in advance" (Magn. 11:1; Trall. 8:1). In this instance they are to be on guard against "beasts in human form," evildoers of the kind mentioned in Ephesians 7:1 and Romans 5:1 (also in Philo, *De Abrahamo* 33; Bauer p. 267). To judge from the allusions to 1 Corinthians 15:30-31 which occur later in this chapter, Ignatius has 1 Corinthians 15:32 in mind ("if . . . I fought with wild beasts"). Christians are not to receive such men (into their houses, 2 John 10-11) or even to meet them (also 2 John; cf. Tit. 3:10); they should, however, pray for them (cf. Eph. 10:1) so that they may repent—difficult (Mark 10:24) though this may be. Jesus Christ, our true life (Eph. 3:2), has the authority over the forgiveness of sins (cf. Mark 2:10). The adjective "true" or "real" (*alēthinos;* Ignatius never used *alēthes*) modifies "life" three other times (Eph. 7:2; 11:1; Trall. 9:2), "suffering" once (Eph. inscr.).

name of Jesus Christ I am enduring all things [2 Tim. 2:10; cf.
1 Cor. 13:7] in order to suffer with him [Rom. 8:17]; and the perfect man himself empowers me [cf. Phil. 4:13].

5 There are some who are ignorant of him and deny him, or
rather have been denied by him; they are advocates of death
rather than of the truth. They were not persuaded by the prophecies or the law of Moses or, thus far, the gospel or our own
individual sufferings. 2. For they have the same opinion about us.
How does anyone help me if he praises me but blasphemes my
Lord and does not acknowledge that he is clothed in flesh? He
who says this has absolutely denied him and is clothed with a

---

Ignatius' mention of "real" life leads him on to discuss the reality
of Jesus' death *and* resurrection—"truly" effected (as in 1:1–2:1;
Magn. 11:1; Trall. 9:1-2).

Ignatius has already expressed the idea that if Christ's sufferings
were only in appearance those who express this view are only in
appearance (2:1; Trall. 10:1), and as in Trallians 10:1, he reveals
that the model for his argument is to be found in 1 Corinthians 15
(especially vs. 30-32). If Christ merely seemed to suffer, why has
Ignatius given himself up to death (1 Cor. 15:31), to fire (perhaps
1 Cor. 13:3, reading "burned"), to sword, to wild beasts (1 Cor. 15:
32)? The answer is that "near sword, near God; with wild beasts,
with God." This statement recalls one in the Gospel of Thomas
(no. 82; also quoted by Origen, PG 13, 531D-32A, and Didymus of
Alexandria, PG 39, 1488D): "He who is near me is near the fire;
he who is far from me is far from the kingdom." J. B. Bauer (in
W. C. van Unnik, *Evangelien aus dem Nilsand,* [Frankfurt, 1960], 123
f.) also adduces the Greek proverb, "He who is near Zeus is near
the lightning." If Ignatius knew the apocryphal saying, he reversed
its meaning; it states that being near Jesus results in persecution
(cf. also no. 16, where Jesus brings "fire, sword, war"), while Ignatius
says that to be persecuted means being near God—because of his
emphasis on the way of the cross, as he goes on to say. He mentions
fire, sword, and wild beasts as various forms which the martyr's
death could take, though he expects the beasts (so Bauer p. 268).
The sentence closely resembles Romans 5:3, though there the horrors
of torture are stressed. It is in the name of Jesus Christ that he is
enduring everything, in order to suffer with him (and be glorified
with him, Paul, Rom. 8:17; cf. Phil. 3:10); the "perfect man" himself
(cf. Paul, Eph. 4:13; Gospel of Philip, p. 103, 11-12; 123, 19-21; 124,
23) gives him strength (Phil. 4:13).

5:1-3. Some "deny" Jesus Christ (cf. Magn. 8:1) and have been
disowned by him (presumably proleptic for the future tense found

corpse. 3. It did not seem good to me to write down their un-believing names; I would rather not even remember them until they repent in regard to the passion, which is our resurrection.

6 Let no one deceive himself: even for heavenly beings and the glory of the angels and the rulers both visible and invisible [Col. 1:16] there is judgment, unless they believe in the blood of Christ; "he who receives, let him receive" [Matt. 19:12]. Office must puff no one up, for faith and love are everything and nothing is preferable to them.

---

in Matt. 10:33; Luke 12:9, also 2 Tim. 2:12; cf. Mark 8:38; Luke 9:26). His language may owe its form to the Pauline "knowing" and "having been known" (1 Cor. 13:12; Gal. 4:9). To deny him means to deny the incarnation (1 John 4:2-3). The deniers are "advocates" for the cause of death, not truth. Prophecies, law, and gospel (cf. on Philad. 5:1-2; Luke 16:29-30), and even the sufferings of Christians (Trall. 10:1; 1 Cor. 15:32) have not persuaded them that Jesus was incarnate.

These men do not understand the reality or the sacrificial signifi-cance of Christian martyrdom (Trall. 10:1). They praise Ignatius (Trall. 4:1) but for the wrong reasons, for they deny Christ's being "clothed in flesh" (cf. Clement, *Str.* 5, 34, 1; Bauer p. 268) and there-fore themselves are "clothed with a corpse," a dead body incapable of resurrection.

Like most New Testament writers and 1 Clement, Ignatius has not named his adversaries; he wishes he might not even remember the names until they repent—as he has said in 4:1. There he refers to Jesus as "our true life" (cf. Trall. 9:2); here he develops the paradox more fully: his passion produces, and therefore is, our resurrection (Magn. 5:2; Trall. inscr.; 11:2; Philad. inscr.).

6:1. "No one should deceive himself"—Ignatius uses a formula of the Cynic-Stoic diatribe, already often employed by the apostle Paul (e.g., 1 Cor. 6:9); elsewhere in Ignatius the phrase occurs in Ephesians 5:2 (cf. Eph. 16:1; Magn. 8:1; Philad. 3:3).

There is a judgment (condemnation) for all who do not "believe in the blood of Christ." What this means is not, as some Monophysites supposed, believing that Christ's blood is God's. Ignatius is simply using "blood" as equivalent to the passion (5:3) or the death of Christ. What he means here is what he says in Trallians 2:1: "by believing in his death you might escape dying." If he is using Paul's Romans 3:25 as a stylistic model ("through faith, in his blood") he is making a mis-take, since Paul's clauses are co-ordinate, not consecutive, though his view is shared by the King James Version and the Book of Common Prayer.

C. Warning against Docetic practice (6:2–9:1)

2. Observe well those who hold heterodox views about the grace of Jesus Christ which came to us—how opposite they are to God's purpose. For love they have no regard, none for the widow, none for the orphan, none for the distressed, none for men imprisoned or released, none for the hungry or thirsty.

7 They abstain from Eucharist and prayer because they do not acknowledge that the Eucharist is the flesh of our Savior Jesus

---

To show how inclusive the range of condemnation will be, Ignatius mentions "heavenly beings" such as "the glory of the angels" (cf. Jude 8; 2 Pet. 2:10) and insists that they must believe. For a judgment of angels compare 1 Corinthians 6:3. (Not all Christians should speculate about such matters, however; cf. on Trall. 5:1-2 and, for the Gospel source of that passage, Matt. 19:10-11.)

Office should exalt no one—angels, rulers visible or invisible (cf. Col. 1:16, as in Trall. 5:2), perhaps some presbyters and deacons?—for nothing is preferable to faith and love (so Magn. 1:2; peace, Eph. 13: 2; Jesus Christ, Magn. 7:1; unity, Polyc. 1:2).

6:2. Heterodox opinions, held by men who are opposed to the purpose of God (which involves episcopal order, Eph. 3:2; Philad. inscr.), are identified as "about the grace of Jesus Christ which came to us" (cf. John 1:17). What Ignatius means is that they do not perform the works of love through which grace is expressed. Grace is actualized, so to speak, in love and the works of love. For their content compare James 1:27 and Matthew 25:34-36. Lightfoot pp. 304-306 (cf. Bauer p. 269) cites many passages from the New Testament and other early Christian writings to show that care for widows, orphans, prisoners, and the poor was regarded as a primary obligation of Christians. For widows compare Smyrnaeans 13:1, and see on Polycarp 4:1; in general, Ephesians 10:2-3. It is from his own experience that Ignatius knows of the neglect of prisoners (Philad. 6:3).

7:1-2. The heterodox not only abstain from works of charity (6:2) but also refrain from participating in orthodox Christian worship: Eucharist (Eph. 13:1; Philad. 4:1) and common prayer (Eph. 5:2; Magn. 7:1; 14:1). Similarly in the Gospel of Thomas (sayings 5 and 14) both prayer and almsgiving are rejected; in the Gospel of Philip there is evidently a Eucharist (saying 68) but the flesh of Jesus "is the logos" (saying 23). Ignatius does not indicate whether or not his opponents have a Eucharist of their own (but cf. 8:1). In any event, they do not regard the Eucharist as Jesus' flesh (cf. Rom. 7:3; Philad. 4:1; like Justin, *Apology* 1, 65-66, he uses the word of the Eucharistic bread) —which "suffered for our sins" (perhaps a formula, since the word

Christ which suffered for our sins, which the Father raised up by
his goodness. Those who deny God's gift are dying in their squab-
bles; it would be better for them to love so that they may rise.
2. It is fitting to keep away from such men and not to speak
about them either privately or publicly, but to pay attention to
the prophets and especially to the gospel, in which the passion
has been explained to us and the resurrection has been accomplished. Flee from divisions as the beginning of evils.

8 All of you are to follow the bishop as Jesus Christ follows the
Father, and the presbytery as the apostles. Respect the deacons as
the command of God. Apart from the bishop no one is to do
anything pertaining to the church. A valid Eucharist is to be de-
fined as one celebrated by the bishop or by a representative of
his. 2. Wherever the bishop appears, the whole congregation is
to be present, just as wherever Jesus Christ is, there is the whole

---

"sins" occurs only here; cf. Bultmann, "Ignatius und Paulus," *Studia
Paulina J. de Zwaan* [Haarlem, 1951], 41, n. 2) and was raised by the
Father's goodness (Magn. 9:2–10:1). Ignatius' association of "flesh"
with "resurrection" in this context is Johannine (John 6:51-58); cf.
Maurer pp. 38-40 and, somewhat differently, H. Koester in *Zeitschrift
für Theologie und Kirche* 54 (1957), 56-69. The heterodox oppose
God's gift and perish while they dispute (cf. Eph. 18:1, based on 1 Cor.
1:20). They should instead love in order to rise (cf. 1 John 2:10-11;
3:14).

Christians must in turn keep away from (the same word as that used
in 7:1) such men (Trall. 6:1; Philad. 3:1) and not even speak about
them, but pay attention to the (Old Testament) prophets and "especially to the gospel" (Philad. 9:2), since it contains the passion and the
resurrection (Philad. 8:2; 9:2). "Flee from divisions" (Philad.
7:2) as the beginning or root of evils (love of money root of evils, 1
Tim. 6:10; beginning of evils, Polycarp, Phil. 4:1).

8:1–2.   Freedom from divisions is ensured by following the bishop
and the presbytery, for the bishop is analogous to the Father and the
presbytery to the apostles who "followed" him. For the bishop as the
Father see Magnesians 6–7; 13:2; Trallians 3:1; for the presbytery as
the apostles, Magnesians 6:1; Trallians 2:2; 3:1 (reversed in Philad.
5:1). Respect for the deacons is also important, for their commands
are equivalent to God's. The authority of the bishop is the most important of all. No Eucharist is valid unless celebrated by him or by
his appointee (cf. 1 Clem. 41); this passage suggests that the heterodox
had their own Eucharist (Lightfoot p. 306).

Church. It is not right either to baptize or to celebrate the agape apart from the bishop; but whatever he approves is also pleasing to God—so that everything you do may be secure and valid.

9   Furthermore, it is reasonable for us to become sober while we still have time to repent toward God. It is good to know God and the bishop. He who honors the bishop has been honored by God; he who does anything without the bishop's knowledge worships the devil.

Meetings are to be held where and when the bishop chooses—just as "wherever Jesus Christ is, there is the *katholikē ekklēsia*." This is the first occurrence of the adjective *katholikos* in Christian literature. Later it means "Catholic" but here means "catholic" in the sense of "whole," "entire," or "general." Elsewhere in second-century literature it is used of the "general" resurrection (Justin, *Dialogue* 81, 4; Theophilus, *Ad Autol.* 1, 13), of "universal" covenants by Irenaeus (*Adv. haer.* 3, 11, 9), and of various items by Clement of Alexandria. Of the Church it occurs four times in the Martyrdom of Polycarp (inscr.; 8:1; 16:2; 19:2), once in the Muratorian fragment, and once in Clement. Polycarp may be called "bishop of the Catholic church in Smyrna" (Mart. Polyc. 16:2) in opposition to a non-Catholic group, but this is uncertain; even when the word becomes more "technical," it always retains the sense of "universal." The "technical" use may be Gnostic in origin; Gnostics called members of the universal Church *communes et ecclesiasticos* (Irenaeus, *Adv. haer.* 3, 15, 2; but *communes* probably translates *koinous*). For Ignatius the word primarily means "universal." But since "Church" involves orthodoxy, "universal Church" obviously has doctrinal and organizational implications.

Apart from the bishop (or his appointee) neither a baptism nor an "agape" can be conducted. It is not clear that in Ignatius' time there was an agape separate from the Eucharist; perhaps it provided the usual setting for the Eucharist.

What the bishop approves is pleasing to God, partly because he is analogous to the Father (8:1), partly perhaps because his decisions, like those of the apostles, are ratified in heaven (cf. Matt. 18:18-20, alluded to in Eph. 5:2; John 20:21-23, alluded to in Eph. 6:1). For the relation of this passage to Matthew 18:20 see M. Goguel in *Revue d'histoire et de philosophie religieuses* 18 (1938), 319.

9:1.   The figurative use of "becoming sober," not uncommon in the New Testament and among Graeco-Roman writers, is found only here among the Apostolic Fathers. The expression translated "while we still have time" is different from a similar phrase in Galatians 6:10; there the word "still" does not occur and we must translate, "as we

D. Ignatius' thanksgiving (9:2–10:2)

2. May all things, then, be abundant for you in grace, for you are worthy. You have refreshed me in every respect; may Jesus Christ refresh you. You loved me when I was both absent and present. God is your reward, and if you endure everything for him you will attain to him.

10 You did well when you received Philo and Rheus Agathopus, who have followed me for the word of God, as deacons of God; they give thanks to the Lord on your behalf because you refreshed them in every way. Nothing will be lost for you. 2. My spirit is devoted to you, as are my bonds, which you neither treated haughtily nor despised [cf. 2 Tim. 1:16]. The perfect hope, Jesus Christ, will not despise you.

---

have occasion." In this instance Ignatius is more eschatologically minded than Paul. To "know" the bishop is to honor him; Bauer p. 271 compares 1 Thessalonians 5:12. On expressions like "he who honors . . . has been honored" see on Ephesians 2:2; also John 12:26.

Bauer (*Rechtgläubigkeit und Ketzerei im ältesten Christentum* [Tübingen, 1934], 73) suggested that this passage points toward the existence of a Gnostic counterbishop in Smyrna. In order to provide evidence, he had to translate the inscription of Polycarp to the Philippians, not as "Polycarp and the presbyters with him" (so commentary, 285) but as "Polycarp and the presbyters on his side" (E. Fascher in *New Testament Studies* 9 [1962-63], 36, not only misquotes but also provides no evidence to support the new translation). The "Gnostic counterbishop" owes his existence not to this passage but to Bauer's imagination.

9:2. May grace abound (cf. Paul, Rom. 5:15), for the Smyrnaeans are worthy because of their "refreshment" of Ignatius (see on Eph. 2:1). They have loved him; their reward will be God, and attaining to him through endurance.

10:1-2. Unlike some of the Philadelphians (Philad. 11:1), all the Smyrnaeans received and "refreshed" the messengers from Antioch. Nothing of what they did will be lost from their account; they have performed "an eternal deed" (Polyc. 8:1).

Ignatius is offering his spirit and his bonds as a sacrifice on behalf of the Smyrnaeans (cf. Eph. 8:1; 21:1; Trall. 13:3; Polyc. 2:3; 6:1), for they were not ashamed of his bonds (cf. 2 Tim. 1:8, 16); therefore Jesus Christ, "the perfect hope" (see on Eph. 21:2), will not be ashamed of them (Mark 8:38; Luke 9:26).

E. The church of Smyrna and the church of Antioch (11:1-3)

11 Your prayer reached the church which is at Antioch in Syria. I came from there in bonds most seemly to God and thus salute all men; not that I am worthy to come from there, since I am the least of them, but by God's will I was judged worthy, not on the ground of my conscience but by God's grace [1 Cor. 15:8-10], which I pray will be given me fully so that by your prayer I may attain to God. 2. So, then, that your work may be complete both on earth and in heaven, it is fitting, for God's honor, for your church to appoint a godly delegate to go to Syria in order to congratulate them on being at peace and on having recovered their proper greatness and on having their proper constitution restored. 3. It appeared to me to be a deed worthy of God for you to send one of your people with a letter so that he may join in glorifying the tranquillity which by God's will has come to them, because through your prayer they have reached harbor. For if you desire to do well, God is ready to help.

11:1–3. The Smyrnaeans' prayer (cf. Philad. 10:1; Polyc. 7:1) has affected the situation of the church at Antioch and has made Ignatius proud to greet all men as an Antiochene Christian in "most Godworthy" (Magn. 1:2; Smyrn. inscr.; Polyc. 7:2) bonds. In expressing his unworthiness to be one of them he paraphrases 1 Corinthians 15:8-10 more fully than elsewhere and prays that the grace he has already, like Paul, received may be "perfectly" given to him (cf. "perfect hope," 10: 2). Ignatius uses words related to perfection (*teleios*, etc.) thirteen times, eight of them in Smyrnaeans presumably because of his close ties with the church there. He hopes by their prayer to attain to God (cf. Eph. 1:2; Magn. 14:1; Rom. 8:3; Philad. 5:1; Polyc. 7:1).

The delegate is to go to Syria—more precisely, to Antioch—and congratulate the Christians there on (1) being at peace once more, (2) having recovered either (*a*) their proper greatness or, more specifically, (*b*) their original size or numbers, and (3) having had restored to them either (*a*) their "constitution," that is, their organizational form, or (*b*) "their own corporate life" (Richardson, *Early Christian Fathers* [Philadelphia, 1953], 116). The meaning of the first point is clear enough, for Ignatius goes on to speak of their newly given tranquillity and their arrival in a haven—as contrasted with being tossed by the sea's waves and winds (cf. C. Bonner in *Harvard Theological Review* 34 [1941], 49-67). The second two suggest questions. Does *megethos* mean size or greatness for Ignatius? Probably the latter, to judge from the Ephesians inscription and Romans 3:3. What does he mean by the word *sōmateion* (Florence MS, Berlin papyrus; Lightfoot, Lake, Bihl-

F. Final greetings (12:1–13:2)

12 The love of the brothers at Troas greets you. From there I am writing you by Burrhus, whom you, together with your brothers the Ephesians, sent with me; he has refreshed me in every way. Would that all imitated him, for he is an embodiment of the service of God. Grace will reward him in every way. 2. I salute the bishop, worthy of God, and the presbytery, fit for God, and my fellow slaves the deacons and all of you, individually and together, in the name of Jesus Christ and in his flesh and blood,

---

meyer) or *sōmation* (interpolated version, Zahn, Bauer)? First of all, it should be noted with Bauer 272 that Ignatius knows the Pauline image of the Church as a body, indeed the body of Christ. The cross was an "ensign" for his saints and believers, both Jewish and Gentile, "in the one body of his Church" (Smyrn. 1:2; cf. Paul, Eph. 2:16, "in one body"). Either *sōmateion* or *sōmation* must involve something characteristic of the *sōma*, the body. Now from Ignatius' own words earlier in Smyrnaeans it is evident that this is primarily unity, as is the case in Paul's letters. But if we consider 1 Corinthians, his favorite Pauline epistle, we see that it is a unity in diversity, held together under the leadership of the ministry. We should incline, therefore, in view of Ignatius' known concern for this matter, to regard *megethos* as meaning greatness and the word related to body as meaning "constitution," in the sense that church order (as Ignatius views it) has now been restored. There was perhaps some question as to whether or not there would be a legitimate bishop of Antioch after Ignatius.

It would therefore be a deed worthy of God (cf. Polyc. 8:1) for them to send a delegate with a letter from the community (Polyc. 8:1) to "glorify" (the Name, Philad. 10:1; the Smyrnaeans' love, Polyc. 7:2) the divine tranquillity present at Antioch. Since the word *eudia* also means "fair weather," Ignatius goes on to mention the "harbor" (see Polyc. 2:3) the Antiochenes are now reaching. Since they are perfect, the Smyrnaeans must have perfect thoughts or plans (based on Paul's words in Phil. 3:15). God is always ready to help (cf. 2 Clem. 15:4).

12:1–2. Ignatius is extremely grateful for the services of the Ephesian deacon Burrhus (Eph. 2:1; Philad. 11:2) and urges all to imitate him, just as Paul urged the Thessalonians to imitate him and the other disciples (1 Thess. 1:6; 2 Thess. 3:7, 9; see also Heb. 13:7). On the imitation motif see on Philadelphians 7:2; on "refreshing" see on Ephesians 2:1. Grace will reward Burrhus as it has rewarded churches and individuals and will also be with Polycarp (Polyc. 8:2; cf. 1:2).

Ignatius greets the church's ministers and the whole congregation, laying emphasis on their unity in Jesus Christ and in his flesh and blood (presumably with a Eucharistic overtone; cf. Rom. 7:3; Philad.

his passion and resurrection both fleshly and spiritual, in union with God and with you. Grace be to you, mercy, peace, endurance forever.

13 I salute the households of my brothers with their wives and children, and the virgins who are called widows. Farewell in the

---

4:1) and in his passion and resurrection (Eph. 20:1; Magn. 11:1; Philad. inscr.; 9:2; Smyrn. 5:3; 7:2), fleshly and spiritual (Eph. 7:2; Magn. 13:1; Smyrn. 13:2; Polyc. 1:2; 2:2), in union with God (cf. Polyc. 8:3) "and with you" (as members of the one body, cf. 1:2). For the benediction "grace, . . . mercy, peace" see 1 Tim. 1:2; 2 Tim. 1:2; 2 John 3; Ignatius characteristically adds "endurance." On deacons as fellow slaves see on Ephesians 2:1.

13:1–2.   Ignatius divides those whom he is greeting at Smyrna into two groups: houses (households) consisting primarily of men but also of their wives and children, and "the virgins who are called widows." The best explanation of the latter group is probably that given by Bauer pp. 273-274 (so also E. Fascher in *New Testament Studies* 9 [1962-63], 36): there are vacancies on the official list of widows (cf. 1 Tim. 5:9; Polycarp, Phil. 4:3) and they are being filled by (older) women who have never been married. The church is thus providing financial support for the elderly whether married or not. Ignatius mentions widows only in letters to the Christians of Smyrna, but this fact does not prove anything about the special situation there; he knows Smyrna better than the other cities and has doubtless been impressed by the prevalence of widows.

Did he write "Farewell in the power of the Father" (*patros*, abbreviated *prs*) or "Farewell in the power of the Spirit" (*pneumatos*, *pns*)? The Latin and Armenian translations read the former; the Greek versions read the latter. Lightfoot p. 324 notes that the expression "the power of God the Father" occurs in Magnesians 3:1. But one would suppose that if Ignatius could speak of "the power of Jesus Christ" (Eph. 11:2) or "the power of faith" (Eph. 14:2), he could speak of the power of the Spirit. Bihlmeyer's parallel is inconclusive, for Ignatius is sometimes repetitious, sometimes not.

Philo the Cilician deacon joined Ignatius at Troas (see Philad. 11:1; Smyrn. 10:1).

Tavia is otherwise unknown and the name does not occur elsewhere (for Tavius and Taouis see Bauer p. 274). Alce is mentioned in Polycarp 8:3 and probably in Martyrdom of Polycarp 17:2. For individual greetings see Polycarp 4:2; 8:2; 3 John 15.

The special salutations in Ignatius' letters reach their maximum in chapters 11–13 and in Polycarp 8:2-3. In Ephesians there were no such greetings, presumably because many Ephesian leaders were with him at Smyrna (Eph. 2:1). To the Magnesians (15:1) Ignatius sends the

power of the Spirit. Philo, who is with me, salutes you. 2. I salute
the household of Tavia, and I pray for her to be established in
faith and love both fleshly and spiritual. I salute Alce, a name
dear to me, and the incomparable Daphnus, and Eutecnus, and
all others individually. Farewell in the grace of God.

---

salutations of the Ephesians and of other churches, writing in Pauline
fashion (Rom. 16:16; 1 Cor. 16:19-20; 2 Cor. 13:12). He himself salutes the Trallians (12:1), as does the love of the Smyrnaeans and the
Ephesians (Trall. 13:1). In Romans 9:3 the salutation is given by his
spirit and by the love of the churches which have received him. Writing
from Troas, he sends the love of the brethren there to the Philadelphians (11:2) and the Smyrnaeans (12:1), again in a Pauline manner
(cf. Phil. 4:21-22; also Tit. 3:15; Heb. 13:24; 1 Pet. 5:13; 2 John 13).
He includes greetings from the Cilician deacon Philo to the Smyrnaeans (13:1), just as Paul conveys greetings from others in his letters
(Rom. 16:21-23; 1 Cor. 16:20; Col. 4:10-12, 14; Philem. 23-24; cf.
2 Tim. 4:21; 1 Pet. 5:13).

POLYCARP

OUTLINE

Salutation (1:1)
A. Exhortation to the bishop (1:2–3:2)
B. The bishop's specific duties (4:1–5:2)
C. The duties of the Smyrnaean Christians (6:1-2)
D. The church of Smyrna and the church of Antioch (7:1–8:1)
E. Final greetings (8:2-3)

Polycarp

Salutation

Ignatius, also called Theophorus, to Polycarp, bishop of the church of the Smyrnaeans (or rather, one who has God the Father and the Lord Jesus Christ as his bishop), abundant greeting.

1 Welcoming your godly mind which is fixed as on an immovable rock [Matt. 7:24-25], I glory exceedingly that I was judged worthy of seeing your blameless face, by means of which I would have pleasure in God.

A. Exhortation to the bishop (1:2–3:2)

2. I exhort you, by the grace with which you are clothed, to press forward on your course and to exhort all men so that they may

---

Salutation. This very brief inscription omits all the honorific expressions that Ignatius has provided in letters to churches; praise of Polycarp is provided only in 1:1. The idea that Polycarp has a "bishop" or "overseer" above him is already expressed in Magnesians 3:1 (the Father is "bishop of all"), Magnesians 3:2 (visible bishop correlated with invisible), and Romans 9:1 (Syrian church has God as shepherd, Jesus Christ and the Romans' love as bishop).

1:1. Ignatius "welcomes" or "acknowledges" (Eph. 1:1; Trall. 1:2) the mind (or counsel or even "attitude") of Polycarp, which is set in God (it is God's, 8:1) as on immovable rock (cf. Matt. 7:24-25; Luke 6:48), and he glories exceedingly (*hyperdoxazō* only here; *doxazō* elsewhere eight times) because he was deemed worthy (here only of what Ignatius has already received, but cf. Magn. 1:2) of (seeing) Polycarp's "blameless" (cf. Smyrn. inscr., "blameless spirit") face, which he would like to enjoy (cf. 6:2; Eph. 2:2; Magn. 2:1; 12:1; even the beasts, Rom. 5:2) in God—perhaps the communion anticipated on earth, to be fulfilled when he attains to God.

1:2–3. Ignatius exhorts Polycarp, by the grace with which he is clad (a Pauline type of expression, cf. 1 Cor. 15:53-54; Gal. 3:27; Rom. 13:14; Col. 3:10; Eph. 4:24), to press forward on his course (cf.

be saved. Vindicate your office with all care both fleshly and
spiritual. Think upon unity, than which nothing is better. Lift
up all men, as the Lord lifts you; put up with all in love, as you
actually do. 3. Be diligent in unceasing prayers; ask for more
understanding than you have; watch with a sleepless spirit. Speak
to each individual after the example of God; bear the sicknesses
[Matt. 8:17] of all, as a perfect athlete. Where the labor is greatest, the gain is great.

2 If you love good disciples, it is no credit to you [Luke 6:32];
instead, bring the more troublesome into subjection by gentle-

---

Acts 13:25; 20:24) and to exhort all men, so that they may be saved—
also by grace (Paul, Eph. 2:5, 8). The counsel to "vindicate" Polycarp's
episcopal "office" (cf. Magn. 6:1) with "diligence" (the first and third
words here only in Ignatius' letters) may be a bit of gnomic wisdom
which Ignatius Christianizes by adding "spiritual and carnal" (in his
letters "carnal" or "fleshly" never appears apart from "spiritual").
Polycarp is to be intent on unity, as Ignatius himself is (Philad. 8:1),
and as the Philadelphians especially ought to be (7:2); indeed, unity
is God himself (Trall. 11:2), and nothing is better than it (cf. Eph.
13:2; Magn. 7:1). Polycarp must therefore bear the burdens (Gal. 6:2)
or weaknesses (Rom. 15:1) of all, as the Lord "bears" him (cf. on
Eph. 2:2); he must "bear with" all "in love" (a reminiscence of Paul,
Col. 3:13; note the context), as he actually does (see on Eph. 8:1).
  He must be "diligent" in "unceasing prayers" (1 Thess. 5:17 with
1 Cor. 7:5). He must ask for more insight than he has (cf. Hermas,
Sim. 5, 4, 3-4), and he must keep his eyes open (in prayer, Col. 4:2);
perhaps Ignatius means that Polycarp's spirit is ready, though his
flesh is weak (Matt. 26:41; Mark 14:38). He is to address all individually (cf. 2:1) just as God does (cf. Magn. 6:2). He is to "bear the
sicknesses" of all (Isa. 53:4 as quoted in Matt. 8:17) as a (or the)
perfect athlete (see below). The words about toil and gain recall 1
Corinthians 3:8 but may be proverbial; cf. J. M. Cotterill, *Modern
Criticism and Clement's Epistles to Virgins* (Edinburgh, 1884), 90,
n. 1.
  2:1–3. "If you love those who love you, what credit is that to you?"
is a saying of Jesus recorded in Luke 6:32 and copied in 2 Clement
13:4; Ignatius alludes either to Luke or to oral tradition (Koester p.
44). Ignatius adapts it by urging Polycarp to deal with the "more
pestilent" (compare "sicknesses" 1:3) with gentleness (a divine attribute, 6:2). He then proceeds to quote two medical tags used by contemporary rhetoricians (e.g., Quintilian, *Institutiones Oratoriae* 4, 2,
84; Plutarch, *De audiendo* 9, p. 42c).
  This saying, again, looks like a modification of what we find in

ness. "Not all wounds are healed by the same plaster." "Relieve convulsions by moist applications." 2. "Be prudent as the serpent" in every matter "and sincere as the dove" [Matt. 10:16] always. You are both fleshly and spiritual for this reason, that you may deal gently with what appears before your face; but ask that invisible things may be made manifest to you so that you may lack nothing and abound in every gift of grace. 3. The occasion calls upon you to attain to God, just as pilots seek winds and the storm-tossed sailor a harbor. Be sober, as God's athlete; the prize is imperishability and eternal life, as you have already been persuaded. In everything I am devoted to you—I and my bonds which you loved.

3 Do not let those who seem plausible but teach strange doctrine buffet you. Stand firm as a hammered anvil. Great athletes are battered, but yet they win. Especially for God's sake we must endure everything so that he may put up with us. 2. Be more

---

Matthew 10:16, whether from "free tradition" (Koester p. 42) or from Ignatius' memory of what he had read. He urges Polycarp to use both his physical and his spiritual faculties so that he may lack no spiritual gift (cf. 1 Cor. 1:7, alluded to in Smyrn. inscr.).

The circumstances make demands (a common Greek expression, Lightfoot p. 339) just as winds do upon a pilot (Ignatius actually says the pilots make demands on winds, presumably mixing his metaphor) and a storm-tossed sailor seeks a harbor (on this metaphor see on Smyrn. 11:3). Lake's suggestion that "possibly something has dropped out of the text" is unnecessary. As the metaphor shifts again, Polycarp becomes an athlete (a common idea among Stoics and early Christians). The prize is "imperishability and eternal life" (cf. Eph. 17:1; Magn. 6:2; Philad. 9:2; Eph. 18:1)—a combination of Pauline and Johannine expressions. Ignatius finally reminds Polycarp of their close personal ties, using the sacrificial word *antipsychon* (see on Eph. 21:1).

3:1–2. Here the athletic metaphor is continued; for the apostles as athletes compare 1 Clement 5 and commentary. The goal of enduring everything is also expressed in Smyrnaeans 4:2; 9:2 (cf. 2 Tim. 2:10); on reciprocity see on Ephesians 2:2.

Polycarp should be more diligent than he is (the theme of chs. 1–4), since Ignatius has already urged the Ephesians (5:3; 10:3; 13:1), the Magnesians (6:1; 13:1), and the Philadelphians (4:1) to diligence in matters of unity. Specifically, he is to note the (signs of the) times or seasons (Matt. 16:2-3; Luke 12:56; cf. Eph. 11:1). He is to look for (as the prophets did, Magn. 9:2) the coming of God, the one who is beyond the present moment. When Ignatius speaks of looking for,

diligent than you are. Understand the times. Wait for him who
is above a moment of time—
  eternal,
  invisible, for our sake visible,
  intangible,
  inpassible, for our sake passible—
him who in every way endured on our behalf.

B. The bishop's specific duties (4:1–5:2)

4 Do not let the widows be neglected; after the Lord, you must
be their guardian. Nothing is to be done without your approval,

---

or expecting, God he obviously has the coming of Jesus Christ in mind
(alluded to only here). He therefore combines a list of God's attributes
(parallel from Plutarch in Bauer p. 277) with statements about the
work of Christ. The list strongly resembles a declaration set forth in
the *Kerygma Petri* (Clement of Alexandria, *Str.* 6, 39, 2-3) and is
undoubtedly based on contemporary Christian teaching about God
(cf. W. C. van Unnik in *Theologische Zeitschrift* 17 [1961], 166-174),
who "made the beginning and controls the end; the Invisible, who sees
all; uncontained, who contains all, without needs, whom all need and
for whom they exist; inconceivable, eternal, imperishable, uncreated."
Ignatius varies his phrasing, sometimes adding paradoxes about what
Christ did "for us" (he does not add "tangible for us" because this
point has already been made in Smyrn. 3:2) and concluding with
Christ's endurance; like "suffering," Ignatius can use this word either
of Christ's work or his own. Tatian provides a similar paradox when
he speaks of Christ as "the God who suffered" (*Oratio* 13); and Ignatius' words were apparently imitated by Irenaeus (*Adv. haer.* 3, 16, 6;
4, 20, 8).

4:1-3. This chapter is the first of two on the bishop's duties in
relation to the life of the community; it deals with three subjects:
widows, frequent meetings, and slaves.

The care of widows was regarded as important from apostolic times
(Acts 6:1; 9:39, 41; Jas. 1:27; 1 Tim. 5:9-16) onward; it is frequently
mentioned in the Apostolic Fathers, especially as the responsibility of
the bishop (Smyrn. 6:2; Polycarp, *Phil.* 4:3; Hermas, *Sim.* 9, 27, 2; cf.
Justin, *Apology* 1, 67, 6). The bishop is to be their "guardian," perhaps
in a semilegal sense.

Frequent meetings are recommended also in Ephesians 13:1; Didache 16:2; 2 Clement 17:3; and Theophilus, *Ad Autol.* 2, 38.

The problem presented by the presence of both masters and slaves
in the same church was generally solved by telling slaves to remain as
they were (1 Cor. 7:21-22) and urging them to obey and respect their

and you must do nothing without God—as indeed is your practice; stand firm. 2. Meetings should be more frequent; seek out all individually. 3. Do not be haughty toward slaves, whether men or women, but do not let them be puffed up. Let them be slaves, rather, for the glory of God, so that they may obtain a better freedom from God. They must not desire to be set free at the expense of the common fund, lest they be found to be slaves of lust.

5 Flee from evil arts, or indeed preach sermons about them. Tell my sisters to love the Lord and to be content with their husbands, both in flesh and in spirit. Similarly, in the name of Jesus Christ

---

masters (Col. 3:22-25; Eph. 6:5-8; 1 Tim. 6:1-2). The masters were to recognize the common Lord in heaven (Col. 4:1; Eph. 6:9) and should forgive runaways when they return (Philem. 15-17). The Didache (4:10-11) advises masters to avoid bitterness and tells slaves to obey as if they were obeying God (so also Barn. 19:7). The idea of emancipation seems to have been far from the minds of most Christians (Tatian, *Oratio* 11, echoes Paul's words about staying as one is). A passage in 1 Clement 55:2 speaks of "many among us who have delivered themselves to bondage in order to ransom others," but the idea of emancipation is very vaguely presented (if at all), and Clement's echoes of 1 Corinthians 13:3 do not make his language more precise. The first mention of emancipation by the church seems to be found in the late fourth century, in *Apostolic Constitutions* 4, 9, 2.

Ignatius has no sympathy with ideas of emancipation. He regards himself as a slave as compared with the free apostles; his freedom will come through dying and rising in Christ (Rom. 4:3; the language recalls 1 Cor. 9:1; 7:22, and perhaps Rom. 7:1-6). In the present passage he is certainly thinking of 1 Corinthians 7:21. True freedom comes from God, not from men. Those slaves who want to be set free at the church's expense are in danger of being slaves of lust. This is a word Ignatius rarely uses, but when he does, it is always in a bad sense (the verb in Rom. 4:3; 7:1; the noun here and in 5:2). The must be lusting for the world, something he contrasts with speaking of Jesus Christ in Romans 7:1. If Ignatius himself can learn in his bonds to desire nothing, slaves—who are not martyrs—can do no less.

5:1-2. The "evil arts" against which Polycarp is expected to preach may well be equivalent to magic, for which the word is often used; they are not quite the same as the "evil arts" of the devil mentioned in Philadelphians 6:2.

Ignatius' urging Christian women to be thoroughly "content" with their spouses (a word apparently chosen in order to include slaves as well as freemen) is paralleled, as for the expression, in Josephus,

command my brothers to love their wives as the Lord loves the Church [Eph. 5:28-29]. 2. If anyone is able to remain in purity, in honor of the Lord's flesh, he must do so without boasting. If he boasts he is lost, and if it is made known to anyone but the bishop, he has been corrupted. It is fitting for men and women who marry to be united with the bishop's consent, so that the marriage may be related to the Lord, not to lust. Everything is to be done in God's honor.

C. The duties of the Smyrnaean Christians (6:1-2)

6 Pay attention to the bishop so that God will pay attention to you. I am devoted to those who are subject to the bishop, pres-

---

Bell. 2, 116 and Epiphanius, *Ancor.* 104, 8 (Lightfoot p. 348); and for the advice, in *Apostolic Constitutions* 8, 32, 4. Husbands are to love their spouses as the Lord loves the Church. This is almost certainly an allusion to Paul's words in Ephesians 5:29. Similar statements about the mutuality of married life are to be found in Stoic writings and in 1 Corinthians 7:3-4, as well as in Theophilus, *Ad Autol.* 2, 28.

Ignatius is not at all opposed to asceticism, but he believes that those who boast about it destroy its value. The same view is expressed in 1 Clement 38:2, and it is presumably based on the Gospel teaching about almsgiving, prayer, and fasting (Matt. 6:1-18), and Paul's statement on continence as a fruit of the Spirit (Gal. 5:23; cf. 1 Cor. 7:7).

Marriages are to be sanctioned by the bishop. For the notion that the Church definitely has a part to play in marriages and, more precisely, in weddings, see Tertullian, *Ad uxorem* 2, 8, 6; *De monogamia* 11, 1 (L. Godefroy in *Dictionnaire de théologie catholique* IX [Paris, 1927], 2104-2105); and Clement, *Str.* 3, 63 (Bauer). The expression "marriage . . . related to the Lord" also occurs in Clement (*Str.* 3, 83, 3); for "not to lust" see 1 Thessalonians 4:5.

6:1–2. This chapter (as well as 7:1, on another subject) is addressed not to Polycarp personally but to the church as a whole (Lightfoot p. 351), less probably to the presbytery and deacons (Harnack in *Texte und Untersuchungen* 20, 3 [Leipzig, 1900], 80-86).

The first sentence exemplifies the characteristic Ignatian idea of reciprocity, which often expresses the notion of imitating God or Christ. Compare the following examples:

Crocus . . . has refreshed me . . . may the Father . . . refresh him (Eph. 2:1)
Remember me, as Jesus Christ remembers you (Eph. 21:1)
Desire it, so that you may be desired (Rom. 8:1)
Glorify his Name . . . and you too will be glorified (Philad. 10:1-2)

byters, and deacons; and may it turn out for me that I have a portion with them in God. Labor together with one another, strive together, run together, suffer together, rest together, rise up together—as God's stewards and assistants and servants. 2. Be pleasing to him for whom you are soldiers, him from whom you will receive your pay. None of you must be a deserter. Let your baptism serve as a shield, faith as a helmet, love as a spear, endurance as full armor. Your works are your deposits so that you may receive the full sum due you. Therefore be patient with one another in gentleness, as God is with you. May I always have joy in you.

> You received them as the Lord received you (Philad. 11:1)
> . . . The Lord Jesus Christ will reward them (Philad. 11:2)
> He who honors the bishop has been honored by God (Smyrn. 9:1)
> You . . . refreshed me, . . . may Jesus Christ refresh you (Smyrn. 9:2)
> You did not despise . . . Jesus Christ will not despise you (Smyrn. 10:2)
> Lift up all men, as the Lord lifts you (Polyc. 1:2)
> We must endure all things for God so that he may put up with us (Polyc. 3:1)
> Be patient . . . as God is with you (Polyc. 6:2)

Similar in form, but different in meaning, are two more:

> Many things are lacking to us so that we may not lack God (Trall. 5:2)
> Be imitators of Jesus Christ as he is of his Father (Philad. 7:2)

The basic idea is close to that of the sayings of Jesus in Matthew 7:7-11 or Luke 11:9-13.

For the expression "I am devoted" see on Ephesians 21:1; for the biblical term "portion" cf. Matthew 24:51; Luke 12:46; Revelation 21:8 (Lightfoot p. 351). Six verbs describing the common life of Christians (from struggle through suffering to death and resurrection) are followed by three nouns emphasizing the necessity of Christian service (cf. Tit. 1:7; 1 Cor. 3:9; 4:1; 1 Pet. 4:10).

The figure then changes to that of the *militia Christi*, with the use of three Latin words: *desertor, deposita, accepta*. The armor seems to come from Paul's Ephesians 6:13-17, the pay perhaps from observation. Half the money awarded to Roman soldiers was paid them in cash, the rest credited as *accepta*. Deserters lost these deposits.

The Christian soldier is to be pleasing to the one he serves (cf. 2 Tim. 2:4), and all Christians are to be "long-suffering" or "patient" (the verb here only in Ignatius; the noun in Eph. 3:1; 11:1) with one another (a paraphrase of Paul, Eph. 4:2)—as God is with them. Ignatius hopes to have joy in them always (so Eph. 2:2).

P. N. Harrison (*Polycarp's Two Epistles to the Philippians* [Cam-

D. The church of Smyrna and the church of Antioch (7:1–8:1)

7 Since the church at Antioch in Syria is at peace (as I have
been informed) because of your (common) prayer, I have become more encouraged in the freedom from care which God has
given me—provided that I may attain to God through suffering,
so that at the resurrection I may be found to be your disciple.
2. It is fitting, Polycarp most blessed by God, to summon a council most fit for God which will appoint someone whom you
[plural] regard as especially dear to you and zealous, someone
who can be called God's courier, and will judge him worthy to go
to Syria and glorify your zealous love to the glory of God. 3. A
Christian has no authority of his own but spends his time for God.
This is God's work, and yours [plural] as well when you complete
it, for I am confident that by grace you [plural] are ready to do
the good deed appropriate to God. Since I know your [plural]
fervor for the truth, I exhort you with only a few lines.

8 Since I could not write all the churches because I am immediately sailing from Troas to Neapolis, as the will of God en-
joins, you [singular] must write, as one possessing the mind of
God, to the churches ahead of me so that they may do the same
thing. Those which can should send messengers; the others should

---

bridge, Eng., 1936], 23) suggested that this chapter has been mis-
placed and should follow Smyrnaeans 10. This is possible, though there
is of course no manuscript support for such an alteration.
  7:1–3. Ignatius' statement about the peace of the church at Antioch
is repeated from Philadelphians 10:1 (cf. Smyrn. 11:2) and his emphasis on his relation to the Smyrnaeans at the resurrection is like that
stated in Ephesians 11:2.
  As in writing to the Philadelphians (10:1-2; cf. Smyrn. 11:2-3), he
insists upon the importance of sending a delegate to Antioch. This
will be a divine mission and it must be undertaken. The remarkable
oscillation between singular and plural in this section may be due to
the unsettling news which Ignatius has received.
  8:1. Ignatius had expected to write "all the churches" (Rom. 4:1);
now he finds that he cannot do so, since his guards have decided to
take him immediately from Troas to Neapolis, the port on the way
to Philippi (cf. Acts 16:11-12), where there was obviously one of the
churches "ahead" to which letters were to be sent. Polycarp did write
to this church, as we learn from his Philippians 13:1.

send letters through those whom you send. In this way you [plural] will be glorified by an eternal deed, since you [singular] are worthy.

E. Final greetings (8:2-3)

2. I salute all individually, including the wife of Epitropus, her whole household, and her children. I salute my beloved Attalus. I salute the one who will be appointed to go to Syria. Grace will always be with him and with Polycarp who sends him. 3. I bid you farewell always in our God Jesus Christ. May you remain in him, in unity with God and under his care. I salute Alce, a person dear to me. Farewell in the Lord.

8:2–3. Finally, Ignatius greets all the Smyrnaeans individually (cf. 1:3; 4:2), including a woman who, as head of a household, must be either a widow or separated from her husband. His name, though unusual, is a real one, though it could mean "the procurator."

On "our God Jesus Christ" see Introduction. The "care" of God is his "episcopal" oversight (see Rom. 9:1; Magn. 3:1) Alce is also "dear" in Smyrnaeans 13:2, as is Crocus in Romans 10:1. On the form of final salutations see on Smyrnaeans 13:2.

SELECTED LIST OF EDITIONS

(arranged chronologically)

USSHER, J., *Polycarpi et Ignatii Epistolae.* Oxford, 1644.

VOSS, I., *Epistolae genuinae S. Ignatii Martyris.* Amsterdam, 1644.

PETERMANN, J. H., *S. Ignatii Patris Apostolici quae feruntur Epistolae una cum ejusdem Martyrio.* Leipzig, 1849. (Armenian version in notes.)

HARNACK, A., ZAHN, T., and GEBHARDT, O., *Patrum Apostolicorum Opera,* Vol. II, *Ignatii et Polycarpi Epistulae Martyria Fragmenta,* ed. T. Zahn. Leipzig, 1876.

LIGHTFOOT, J. B., See Selected Bibliography.

LAKE, K., *The Apostolic Fathers,* Vol. I. London, 1912.

BIHLMEYER, K., FUNK, F. X., and SCHNEEMELCHER, W., *Die Apostolischen Väter,* Vol. I. Tübingen, 1956.

SELECTED BIBLIOGRAPHY

(Books or articles marked * are usually cited only by the author's name)

BARNARD, L. W., "The Background of St. Ignatius of Antioch," *Vigiliae Christianae* 17 (1963), 193-206.

* BARTSCH, H. W., *Gnostisches Gut und Gemeindetradition bei Ignatius von Antiochien.* Gütersloh, 1940.

* BAUER, W., *Die Briefe des Ignatius von Antiochia und der Polykarpbrief.* Tübingen, 1920.

BROWN, M. P., *The Authentic Writings of Ignatius.* Durham, N. C., 1963.

BULTMANN, R., "Ignatius und Paulus," *Studia Paulina J. de Zwaan.* Haarlem, 1951, 37-51.

CABANISS, A., "Wisdom 18:14 f: An Early Christmas Text," *Vigiliae Christianae* 10 (1956), 97-102.

CAMPENHAUSEN, H. VON, *Die Idee des Martyriums in der alten Kirche.* 2nd ed., Göttingen, 1963.

CHADWICK, H., "The Silence of Bishops in Ignatius," *Harvard Theological Review* 43 (1950), 169-172.

COLSON, J., "Agape chez Saint-Ignace d'Antioche," *Texte und Untersuchungen* 78 (1961), 341-353.

* CORWIN, V., *St. Ignatius and Christianity in Antioch.* New Haven, 1960.

* DANIÉLOU, J., *Théologie du Judéo-Christianisme.* Louvain, 1958.

DAUBE, D., "Τρία μυστήρια κραυγῆς: Ignatius, Ephesians XIX. 1," *Journal of Theological Studies* 16 (1965), 128-129.

DOWNEY, G., *A History of Antioch in Syria.* Cambridge, Mass., 1960.

GOLTZ, E. VON DER, *Ignatius von Antiochien als Christ und Theologe,* Texte und Untersuchungen 12, 3, Leipzig, 1894.

GRANT, R. M., "The Odes of Solomon and the Church of Antioch," *Journal of Biblical Literature* 63 (1944), 363-377.

———, "Hermeneutics and Tradition in Ignatius of Antioch," in E. Castelli, ed., *Ermeneutica e tradizione* (Rome, 1963), 183-201; slightly revised as "Scripture and Tradition in St. Ignatius of Antioch," *Catholic Biblical Quarterly* 25 (1963), 322-335.

* HARRISON, P. N., *Polycarp's Two Epistles to the Philippians.* Cambridge, Eng., 1936.

KLEIST, J. A., *The Epistles of St. Clement of Rome and St. Ignatius of Antioch.* Westminster, Md., 1946.

KNOX, J., *Philemon Among the Letters of Paul.* Chicago, 1935.

141

KOESTER, H., "Geschichte und Kultus im Johannesevangelium und bei Ignatius von Antiochien," *Zeitschrift für Theologie und Kirche* 54 (1957), 56-69.

* ——, *Synoptische Überlieferungen bei den Apostolischen Vätern, Texte und Untersuchungen* 65, Berlin, 1957.

* LIGHTFOOT, J. B., *The Apostolic Fathers. Part II: S. Ignatius. S. Polycarp.* London, 1885, 2d ed., 1889.

* MAURER, C., *Ignatius von Antiochien und das Johannesevangelium.* Zurich, 1949.

MOFFATT, J., "Ignatius of Antioch: A Study in Personal Religion," *Journal of Religion* 10 (1930), 169-186.

——, "An Approach to Ignatius," *Harvard Theological Review* 29 (1936), 1-38.

MOLLAND, E., "The Heretics Combatted by Ignatius," *Journal of Ecclesiastical History* 5 (1954), 1-6.

* PREISS, T., "La mystique de l'imitation du Christ et de l'unite chez Ignace d'Antioche," *Revue d'histoire et de philosophie religieuses* 18 (1938), 197-241.

* RICHARDSON, C. C., *The Christianity of Ignatius of Antioch.* New York, 1935.

——, "The Church in Ignatius of Antioch," *Journal of Religion* 17 (1937), 428-458.

RIESENFELD, H., "Reflections on the Style and the Theology of St. Ignatius of Antioch," *Texte und Untersuchungen* 79 (1961), 312-322.

ROMANIDES, J. S., "The Ecclesiology of St. Ignatius of Antioch," *Greek Orthodox Theological Review* 7 (1961-62), 53-77.

SCHILLING, F. A., *The Mysticism of Ignatius of Antioch.* Philadelphia, 1932.

* SCHLIER, H., *Religionsgeschichtliche Untersuchungen zu den Ignatiusbriefen.* Giessen, 1929; with review by A. D. Nock in *Journal of Theological Studies* 31 (1929-30), 310-313.

SCHOEDEL, W. R., "A Blameless Mind 'Not on Loan' but 'By Nature' (Ignatius, *Trall.* i. 1)," *Journal of Theological Studies* 15 (1964), 308-316.

SHEPHERD, M. H., Jr. "Smyrna in the Ignatian Letters," *Journal of Religion* 20 (1940), 141-159.

SNYDER, G. F., "The Historical Jesus in the Letters of Ignatius of Antioch," *Biblical Research* 8 (1963), 3-12.

* TORRANCE, T. F., *The Doctrine of Grace in the Apostolic Fathers.* Edinburgh, 1948.

A.-G., *A Greek-English Lexicon of the New Testament and Other Early Christian Literature. A translation and adaptation of Walter Bauer's Griechische-Deutsches Wörterbuch zu den Schriften des Neuen Testaments und der übrigen urchristlichen Literatur* (4th revised and augmented edition, 1952). By William F. Arndt and F. Wilbur Gingrich. Chicago, 1957.